GRAVE TALES FROM WALES

More 'Stories in Welsh Stone'

By

Geoff Brookes

Published by

Llyfrau Cambria Books, Wales, United Kingdom.

Cambria Books is a division of

Cambria Publishing Ltd.

Discover our other books at: www.cambriabooks.co.uk

To Kath Rhodes and Ian Mole at Welsh Country Magazine. I thank them both and their colleagues, past and present, most sincerely for their support. Their encouragement and their belief in my work, has made this book possible.

All photographs used were taken by the author, Geoff Brookes.

For more books by Geoff Brookes please visit his website at
https://www.geoffbrookes.co.uk/

Cover Image: Graves at Cwm yr Eglwys in Pembrokeshire

CONTENTS

Introduction

Grave Tales from Wales provides, at last, a sequel to the popular *Stories in Welsh Stone*, my first work about Welsh history. And, as they did in that book, gravestones from across Wales provide a remarkable window into the past. The stories they represent are about the lives of the people who still lie beneath those stones, who still lie beneath your feet, and who still have something to say.

You may touch a grave, and whilst it might appear to be, as the poet Andrew Marvell said, *'a fine and private place,'* you will be a welcome intruder, connecting instantly with the person it represents; you will feel the weight of the story that lies within. Headstones are not untouchable relics behind a security screen; they are physical memories. Your presence, your touch, brings those memories to life.

In this book you will find stories that cannot be ignored; stories of anguish and sorrow, stories of courage and achievement. These are tales from the past that can still speak to us today. There are great events here – the Titanic, the sinking of The Royal Charter, the execution of a King – but there are also terrible murders. And these open a window into the lives of ordinary people, lives that are often overlooked in the historical record.

The stories stretch out from 1680 to 1949, and are arranged, not by theme or date, but by location, and in this way I hope that the book offers a collection of fascinating places to visit – visits that will create a connection between you and the heritage of Wales.

The book was compiled over many years using contemporary newspapers, and of course, by visiting the graves themselves. These stories first appeared as articles in *Welsh Country Magazine* and I am especially grateful for the support and encouragement it has given me over the years - for the faith it placed in my writing and, of course, for the opportunity to explore all these amazing stories. The magazine has graciously given me permission to reproduce the stories that I wrote for them and I thank them for that.

I would also like to thank Chris and his team at Cambria Books for helping me put this book together. Yes, it is a labour of love, but this book is all about the stones. They were here before we were and they will still be there after we have gone. That is what makes them so special. I regard this work as a duty, and I hope the stories in this book that we have rediscovered as we have toured through Wales, will not be forgotten again.

Bassaleg, Gwent
The Murders of Charles and Mary Thomas 1909

I never did do it

Tank Cottage in Bassaleg was a small property, dominated by a large water tank in the front garden. It was the home of Charles and Mary Thomas. He was 82 and she was ten years younger. They had lived on the Tredegar Estate in Newport, where Charles had been a wood cutter but now, just two weeks previously, he had finally retired and the couple had been given use of Tank Cottage.

Bethesda Chapel, Bassaleg

3

On Thursday 11 November 1909 they went to bed, early as usual. But their neighbours didn't see them at all on Friday and became alarmed. Mary hadn't turned up to go shopping in Newport with a friend, as was her habit. So Constable Bale was called and he found a terrible scene when he forced his way into the cottage and went upstairs. Charles and Mary were dead in bed, their heads beaten with a heavy blunt instrument until they were almost unrecognisable. Blood was splattered everywhere. It had been a brutal, frenzied assault on a benign elderly couple.

The police began house-to-house enquiries in the shocked community and searched nearby streams for the murder weapon. Lord Tredegar advised the police to call in bloodhounds. They dug the garden, they drained the water tank but they never found the murder weapon. The police believed that it was a hammer.

Crowds gathered to look at Tank Cottage, taking away twigs from the bushes as souvenirs. The police were sure that the murderer was someone with local knowledge, someone who believed that the recently retired couple had a secret stash of cash. They focused their enquiries on 'The Midnight Wanderer,' someone who was often seen in Bassaleg in the dark. Everyone knew who he was. And when they decided to arrest him on Monday 15 November, they didn't have to look too far, because he'd already been in custody since Saturday, in the police station in Newport.

His name was William Butler, who claimed to be 78 years old and a Crimean War veteran. He described himself as a jobbing gardener and had been summoned to appear in court on Friday 12 November 1909 for harassing Florence West.

Now, Florence was only fifteen years old; she was a domestic servant for the stationmaster at Bassaleg, and Butler wouldn't leave her alone. He followed her everywhere and kept asking her to marry him. This certainly amused the press, but Florrie was understandably afraid of him, and her family had to escort her to

4

and from work. Butler denied accusations that he had insulted her and had threatened to knock her down with a stick if she wouldn't speak to him. He also threatened to kill the stationmaster who was trying to protect her. Butler had been a lodger in the West's house until recently but had moved away to new lodgings with Mrs Doody.

As a result of his predatory behaviour, Butler was bound over to keep the peace, but he chose to go to prison rather than pay any sureties. And so that is where he was when the police officers came to call on Monday morning - in custody at the County Police-station in Newport, waiting to be transferred to Usk Prison.

He denied any suggestion that he was a murderer, of course. He liked the couple. He'd done some work for them. Why should he kill them? He'd been in bed. All night. The police though, were not convinced and began to unravel his carefully constructed alibi. And when you know that the West's lived next door to Charles and Mary Thomas, and that when Butler moved out to lodge with Mrs Doody he had taken a hammer, you can understand the police interest in him. Indeed, a week earlier, when Butler had been presented with the summons for his harassment of Florence, he had told the West's, *'I'll make you sit up. I will ruin this house, and I will bring tears to your eyes before the week is out.'*

On 11 November he made sure Mrs Doody saw him go to bed early but, of course, the police maintained that in reality he had slipped out of the house. A witness claimed to have seen him. The police said that he had previously oiled the garden gate at Tank Cottage so that it made no noise. He then broke a window next to the door, muffling the sound by holding a girl's bodice filled with mud against the glass. Next, he had slipped his hand inside and lifted the latch on the door. He had also worn Mr Doody's boots, which left prints larger than his own shoe size.

The police felt that he had been motivated by a desire to steal money to pay his legal expenses, and also by a burning desire to frame the West family, for he placed the front door key to Tank Cottage on the windowsill of the West's house when he left. They believed that Butler had searched fruitlessly for money downstairs and so went upstairs. When Mary awoke, he battered them both to death. All he found was a small sum of about £5 in coins, which Charles had received as sick pay from a benefit club that he paid into. Butler never found their life savings of £160, hidden in a laundry basket.

He knew the murders were not likely to be discovered until late on Friday 12 November. So early that morning he made sure he was seen in Cardiff. He'd walked there in order, he said, to consult his solicitor, but even in those days Cardiff solicitors were never hot-to-trot at quarter to eight in the morning. He then went by train to Newport and returned to Cardiff in the afternoon to meet his legal expert. And then, as we know, on Saturday he was in the cells.

Butler gave varying accounts of his movements, which were found to be untrue, and he was unable satisfactorily to explain why on Thursday 11 November he had no money but then the next day he was spending freely. He said he had backed the Derby winner, but the bookmaker had no knowledge of any such bet. He hired his solicitor using coins in the same denominations as those in Charles' sick pay; he had generously tipped a waitress in a café.

The police lacked direct evidence of his guilt. He seemed to have protected himself from the splattering of the victim's blood, perhaps with a piece of newspaper, but there was circumstantial evidence which persuaded the jury of his guilt. The death sentence was followed by a remarkable scene of raving, shouting, and blasphemy. He had to be restrained as he was taken away.

Butler's previous convictions were also revealed. He had been born in Gloucestershire as Thomas Clements and he was 68, ten years younger than he claimed. He had never been in the Crimea. He had a string of offences for stealing and poaching. In fact, he had spent over twenty years in a variety of prisons, under a variety of aliases. He had once threatened policemen with a revolver.

Naturally, he maintained that he had been framed. After the trial he not only expected to be released but also promised to murder the witnesses who all told lies about him by cutting them to pieces, which even in Newport was considered unacceptable.

His appeal failed and he was hanged in Usk prison on 24 March 1910, still protesting his innocence. *'I never did do it,'* he said.

Following the execution, it was suggested that he might have been responsible for the murder of Mary Hogg in Camberley in 1906. She, too, had been beaten to death with a hammer. Butler had spent time in both Winchester and Oxford Prisons and he seemed to be wandering around the area at the time. He fitted the description provided by Miss Hogg's sister Caroline, who had also been attacked. However, no direct link was ever established.

It is said that Butler now haunts the Tredegar Arms on Caerphilly Road in Bassaleg, stamping on the floorboards in the Lounge Bar where the inquest into the deaths of Mr and Mrs Thomas were held, still protesting.

Tank Cottage was demolished.

Charles and Mary were buried on Tuesday 16 November 1909 in Bethesda Chapel where they worshipped every Sunday. Bethesda Chapel stands on Cefn Road and the grave they share is in the bottom right-hand corner of the cemetery. It is just one amongst many, with nothing to indicate the dreadful story it contains.

We know about it now, though. And suddenly that gravestone looks very different.

Brithdir, Gwynedd
The murder of Sara Hughes 1877

It was a gruesome jigsaw

It is a stretched-out sort of village and there are three cemeteries. We tried all three. It was a wet August day and we had little success in finding her grave. We walked in an aimless fashion around the remaining graves next to a chapel that had recently been converted to a nursery. And then we met him, a nice old gentleman maintaining the fences. He knew the story and, although he was initially reluctant, he opened up. It may have happened over 100 years ago but the memory of such events lies fresh in small communities. They don't much like outsiders poking about, opening up old wounds, parading the kind of shame that a village doesn't need, even after all these years. But ours was a genuine interest. Our intention was to set the record straight and he directed us back to the first cemetery we had looked at and took us to the stone. You can find it under the trees in the corner, as if it is too ashamed to face the bright light of day. We hadn't noticed it, because what we should have been looking for was her father's grave. He was put there to join her, with her mother Margaret next to them. It was Richard Hughes we should have been looking for all along, not Sara. But at least we had found her, the poor unfortunate Sara Hughes. Murdered, dismembered and thrown in a river. A woman remembered for her death, not for her life.

She lived with her sister in a house called Pencraig in Brithdir, near Dolgellau. She supported her family by taking in washing and carrying out casual domestic duties in neighbouring farms. There can be no doubt that Sara was a girl with a reputation. She was unmarried, and with two children and possibly another on the way, she was not regarded as a paragon of virtue. In 1877 she was 36

8

years old and was last seen alive on Thursday 4 June, when she walked down to Dolgellau to see her friend Margaret Williams in Unicorn Lane. She had told her sister that she was going to be late and that after seeing Margaret she was going to visit a friend. She left Unicorn Lane at 9.00pm and walked off up the River Arran along Torrent Walk, and at that point she effectively disappeared.

The alarm was raised the next morning and it is significant that the family immediately suspected foul play. They searched along the River Arran that runs down into Dolgellau but found no trace of her. They could get no support from the authorities. The police believed that she had left for the industrial towns of South Wales, to work in whatever way she could find. A missing person's report was sent to the south but at no point did the police search in the local area with any enthusiasm.

The Hughes family then walked down into Dolgellau and engaged the help of the Town Crier. A group of townspeople formed a search party, with bloodhounds they say, and returned to the river, which was at a very low level throughout June. There was, however, no trace of her. The locals continued to believe for a great many years that the police would have taken the issue much more seriously if it had been a case of salmon poaching.

Yet Sara did turn up, up early in the morning of Monday 16 July 1877 - but in pieces.

After a prolonged drought, there had been heavy rain and those people out early in the morning saw her dismembered corpse floating through Dolgellau. It was a scene from another world. A little girl saw an arm in the water as she crossed the wooden bridge over the Arran in the middle of the town. It was retrieved from where it had lodged against a bridge support. The hand was open and two fingers were covered in the fragments of a bandage. Sara had cut her fingers and her sister had bandaged them. This was an important part of her identification. Lungs and entrails were found and other parts soon turned up. The torso, parts of clothing, a foot

9

still wearing a boot. Then they found the head. It had been battered and abused. Although the hair had been cut off and the eyes gouged out, they knew who it was. Parts of her body continued to appear throughout the morning. In the end they saw that she had been inexpertly carved into twelve separate pieces whilst still clothed. They recovered eleven of them. A piece of a leg was never found.

A new bridge perhaps, but still the same river

If anything was ever going to galvanise the police into action it was this and the pieces were assembled in the Workhouse. It was a gruesome jigsaw, and all that remained of an incomplete life; an incomplete body.

When they were confronted by the body parts of a woman floating through the town, a woman whose disappearance they had previously dismissed, the authorities sprang, finally, into action. A shock ran through the town, a sense of horror and shame that such an awful thing should happen here. It was something strangers did, not something committed by someone you may have passed regularly in the street, someone you might even know.

There was something evil here, and it needed to be purged.

There was an inquest the next day, when her sister confirmed that the body was indeed that of Sara. It cannot have been easy for Margaret to identify the corpse, though she probably agreed to do so to spare her parents the horror. Doctor Williams and Doctor Jones established that death had been caused by an extensive fracture of the skull. The body seemed to be too well preserved to have been in the river for six weeks since her disappearance. The question was, where had the poor girl been?

The inquest was adjourned until 1 August, to allow the police time to start a proper and belated investigation and Sara was buried quietly in the churchyard in Brithdir later that day.

But the police already had an important piece of information. The weather.

Sara could not have been put in the river more than 2 days previously, because the river level had been so low that she would have been seen, especially since the family had themselves searched the river side so thoroughly. The police believed, quite reasonably, that the murderer had thrown the body into the river when the heavy rain came, in the hope that it would wash down the Arran, into the Wnion and then eventually out to sea. It also seemed reasonable to assume that the body would not have been carried far. So they concentrated their inquiries alongside the river. It didn't take them long to work out who was the murderer.

Sara's misfortune had been to establish a relationship with Cadwaladr Jones. He wasn't an uneducated man. He liked reading poetry and copying out hymns. He was married, he had a child and he was 26 years old. He lived in Parc Farm, a mile or so upstream of Dolgellau. It wasn't much of a farm to be honest, a grim cottage

11

where he kept a cow and five sheep. This is why he spent most of his time working as a labourer on other farms. Throughout May and June he had been working on a neighbouring farm called Coed Mwsoglog. He stayed there during the week and only returned to his own home on Saturdays.

Sara was working here too.

Investigations would later indicate that no one ever saw any signs of intimacy between them, but the story that has been passed down in Brithdir is that she was pregnant. Her sister was sure of it. It certainly provided a compelling explanation of what Jones did.

She had left Unicorn Lane in Dolgellau to go and see him, for Jones had, unusually, gone back home on that Thursday. The story goes that his wife wasn't at home that night. So Sara felt confident about walking up to Parc Farm, where perhaps she thought they were going to sort things out. If that was the case, it didn't turn out as she anticipated. Jones was a frightened, married man who had no idea what he was going to do, confronting an older, more experienced woman.

It was clear that the suspicions had always been there. They asked her father who he suspected and he told them; Cadwaladr Jones. The man who found Sara's abused head told the police that on the Monday morning when Sara was being collected from the river, Jones had been apparently fishing in the Arran. Odd behaviour, for he should have been at work, and anyway the river itself was in flood. When told about the body in the river, Jones said that he knew the woman very well.

There was enough here to warrant a very serious visit. So the police went early to Parc Farm and surrounded the building. When Jones came to door, he almost immediately confessed. The horror of what he had done was probably an intolerable burden that he could no longer carry alone. He showed them a pair of blood-stained trousers and he took them to the shabby little cow house at the far end of the garden. Here they found fragments of her clothes. He then showed them where he had buried her in the garden. He gave them a recently sharpened bill hook with a broken handle. He showed them a chopping block.

Sara had arrived to see him. They had argued and he had hit her once with an iron handle from a butter churn or grinding wheel. Then, like many murderers, he was left with the considerable problem of what to do with the body. Initially, he buried her in the garden and then exhumed her when a better idea occurred to him. On Sunday 16 July 1877, in the pouring rain, he chopped up her body in the cowshed. His wife said that he was very busy that day and *'appeared to have something on his mind.'*

You can be sure of that.

Jones went before the Dolgellau magistrates on Thursday and then eventually to Chester Assizes. where he was condemned to death. David Pugh was paid £3 to translate the proceedings into Welsh so that Jones could understand, though the outcome was never in doubt. Thomas Hughes received a great deal more. He was paid £65 for providing the scaffold and the apparatus. The executioner Marwood turned up to do the deed and pronounced the arrangements to be *'the best he had ever witnessed.'*

The execution took place in Dolgellau Gaol at 8.00 am on 23 November 1877. As you can imagine, the press loved every moment. His death was the end of *'a career of secret sinning.'* He was the subject of a great many sermons and lurid warnings. But when the national attention shifted, the story lived on in Brithdir. As does the sense of shame that their local community could have within it a desperate man who could do such a thing.

The best way to find Sara is to leave the A470 and take the B4416 that drops so suddenly and takes you over a narrow bridge across the Afon Clywedog which rushes down to join the Wnion. As you drive into Brithdir you will eventually see the church of St Marc on the right hand side of the road, just before a bend in the road. There is a place to park opposite the church on the left side of the road. Go into the green cemetery and at the back, under the dark trees next to the wall of the church, you will find her. It is her father's grave. 'Robert T Hughes Died 1884.' Sara is named beneath.

Where Sara rests with her father

Bryn Crug, Tywyn, Gwynedd

Mary Jones 1864

Mary Jones His The True Onour of thie Bible.
Bought in the Year 1800 Aged 16th

So much has attached itself to Mary Jones that it is hard to disentangle myth and reality. But what is undoubtedly true is that, for a while, she was the most famous Welsh woman throughout the developing world. Her story was an inspiration, an example. The little Welsh girl without a Bible, who walked 25 miles to Bala, in her bare feet, to get one.

But to understand Mary you have to understand the landscape within which she lived. And you can only do that by going there. Her home was a wild place. As remote a place as you can find.

Drive over the hill from Abergynolwyn, along a single track road that takes you into a beautiful and remote valley, past the ruins of Castell y Bere, the last Welsh castle to fall to Edward 1, and on towards Llanfihangel y Pennant. Here is the low grey chapel that she attended. Follow the road beyond until it ends at a bridge over the Afon Cader, in the shadow of the Cader Idris and this is where she lived, far away from anywhere. The broken walls of the tiny cottage of Tyn y ddol, which she shared with her mother, also called Mary, remain. It is a shell beside the tumbling river, and in front of where the hearth would have been, there is an obelisk with a representation of an open book, a memorial to her endeavour.

Tyn y ddol was her world, a single room. And when you see it you are not surprised that she walked so far. What else could she do?

Tyn y ddol

It was a harsh world into which Mary was born in December 1784, the only child of Jacob and Mary who were weavers. Jacob died in 1789 and after that, the two Marys were left to cope as best they could.

Mary attended religious meetings with her mother from an early age, carrying the lamp that guided them back from the chapel to their remote home. Wherever they wanted to go, they would have to walk the sort of distance that today would seem daunting. But this was Mary's life. A quiet, insular, Welsh-speaking community, that depended upon wool and weaving. There was no expectation that life would ever be anything else. But the world outside their valley was changing and the means by which it was changed was through religion.

The Methodist movement became more prominent in the north, particularly after it recruited the evangelical Anglican

16

clergyman from south Wales, Thomas Charles. He was described as *'The Lord's Gift to the North'* and he played a crucial part in the story of Mary Jones. Because of him, Bala became a centre of the Methodist movement, described disparagingly by Anglicans as the *Methodist's Mecca*. It became a truth universally acknowledged that people were ready to walk a considerable distance to listen to him speak. This is an important detail.

Neither should there be any doubt that Charles did a great deal to improve levels of literacy in the region. Crucially, he established circulating schools. He would employ schoolmasters who would stay in one place for a short time, training a local monitor to continue the work, before moving on. They would teach people to read the Bible and reinforce basic principles of faith. In effect, they were, essentially, missionaries. Their work was then sustained by the Sunday school movement. As a result, religion became the means by which education could be brought to these remote areas.

A consequence of this was that increasing numbers wanted a Welsh language Bible, one that they could read for themselves, at a price that they could afford. How could this increased demand be satisfied?

The answer was found in the creation of the British and Foreign Bible Society in 1804 – and the vehicle he used to market it, was the story of Mary Jones.

The story was remarkably effective and achieved almost mythical status. The original story was carefully embellished and then polished, to be taken around the world. It presented a simple personal challenge to all those who heard it. Can you match the devotion of Mary Jones? It still does.

When Mary was ten years old, a circulating school was established at Abergynolwyn about two miles away and she attended regularly and also at the Sunday school. She was a capable girl and was eager to learn to read. For her, walking along and around that small world of hers, dominated by those huge hills, was completely normal. What alternative was there? And her purpose in walking so regularly to school was to learn to read, so that she would be able to read the Bible and then to memorise it.

There was a copy of the Bible in the church of St Michael's at Llanfihangel y Pennant of course, but the only other one in the area was in a farm called Penybryniau Mawr, about two miles away. She was allowed to go into the parlour to read it and she would go there every week over a period of six years to do so. Soon her motivation changed; what she wanted now was a Bible of her own.

She was given hens and began to sell the eggs to earn the money she needed to buy one. She sold honey; she knitted. There was little money where she lived and it took her six years to save enough. It was truly a case of scraping pennies together. She eventually managed to acquire seventeen shillings, a considerable sum. In fact, the remarkable thing is, I think, that it was not so much her legendary walk to Bala to collect a Bible that was notable; it was that she was able to scrape enough money together to buy one, there at the very end of a valley where no one had any. And for me, that is the most fascinating thing about all this. Whether you have religious belief or not, Mary's story is a remarkable insight into a disappeared rural life.

It was 1800 and, on one of her visits to read the Bible, she met a man on a white horse in particularly heavy rain. It was Thomas Charles. After asking why she was out and about in such bad weather, he told her that he was expecting the delivery of Welsh Bibles from London. She would be able to buy one from him.

This is why she set off over Cader Idris on her barefoot walk to Bala. This was not particularly unusual, for it would be preferable to walk barefoot rather than to wreck her precious clogs. And the walk was one she had done before quite frequently. Mary had walked to Bala on other occasions, overnight on Saturday, in order to arrive in time for Sunday Communion. The idea of being out on the hills in the darkest of nights held no terrors for her. This was her landscape. We would find it wild, dark, threatening. To her and her community, it was normal.

It was a round trip of 50 miles.

When she arrived, she was told that the Bibles had not yet arrived. So she stayed with one of Charles' maids until they were delivered two days later. For her devotion, they gave her three copies to take home. She is reputed to have composed a verse on that triumphant journey.

> *Yes, at last I have a Bible,*
> *Homeward now I needs must go;*
> *Every soul in Llanfihangel*
> *I will teach its truths to know.*

And that really is the end of her part in the story. She slipped back into her small community and embraced her life of poverty and hardship. It was Thomas Charles who saw the possibilities that her story contained.

Her visit made such an impression on Charles that he spoke of her walk at a meeting of the Religious Tract Society in London at the end of 1802. So inspired were they that they formed the British and Foreign Bible Society two years later. Bibles were printed in every available language and taken across the world, and with them went the story of Mary Jones.

But of course the real Mary played no part in this. She was now merely a devotional symbol, and one that was starting to move some distance from reality. And, as her story travelled and grew, so her own life closed in upon itself.

Her own story was initially preserved in the oral history. Towards the end of her long life, she reminisced to a local governess, called Lizzie Rowlands. Mary married a weaver called Thomas Lewis in 1813 and they had six children, though five died in infancy. They moved down to Bryn Crug in 1820, where she supplemented their meagre income by selling honey. The minister of Bryn Crug, Robert Griffith, particularly admired her relationship with the bees. '*She could pick them up in her hands like corn, or oatmeal, without any one of them using its sting to oppose her.*' This was a sign that the bees realised she was engaged in God's work, apparently, for the income she gained from the beeswax she divided between the Bible Society and the Missionary Society, despite her own needs.

She suffered considerably from depression in her later days and died a blind widow in December 1864. The fact that she had memorised large parts of the Bible as a child was of some comfort to her, when she could no longer read. One of her Bibles was on a table by her side when she died, aged 80.

That Bible is now in the Archives of the Bible Society in Cambridge and in the back she wrote

I bought this in the 16th year of my age. I am Daughter of Jacob Jones and Mary Jones His wife, the Lord may give me grace. Amen.

Mary Jones His The True Onour of the Bible. Bought in the Year 1800 Aged 16th.

The second Bible is in the University of Aberystwyth and the third she was given has disappeared, taken, perhaps, by her only surviving child, John, when he emigrated to the anonymity of America.

In Bala there is a statue to Thomas Charles but there is no representation of Mary anywhere. Who she was, has always been less important than what she did and what it was used to represent. What ever happened in the rest of her hard life, it was that walk which fixed her place in history forever. It became an epic Sunday school story. A little girl walking such a long way to collect a Bible? Are you as worthy as her?

In Bryn Crug, north east of Tywyn, you must turn right off the main road, the A493, in the centre of village, immediately after you have crossed the river. There, in front of you on the right, you will see the Bethlehem Methodist Chapel. Follow the slate sign that directs you around the back and you will see Mary's grave, surrounded by railings. It was erected by the Sunday schools of Merionethshire and is much grander than anywhere she lived when she was alive. The original stone lies on the ground and above it a new one shines, in English and in Welsh. *'In memory of Mary Jones.'* She will never be forgotten. A version of her story will continue. But as time passes on we get further and further from the truth of what she did.

The Bethlehem Methodist Chapel, Bryn Crug

Thomas Charles died in 1814 and is buried in St. Bueno's Church Llandycil, on the shore of Lake Bala, in a large chest tomb at the east side. We are told of '*his indefatigable endeavours when in London to procure a supply of the Holy Scriptures for the use of his native countrymen.*' He was ready to exploit Mary's story for what he believed was a greater good. And as a result, the name of Mary Jones is far more well-known than his. But I don't suppose that would trouble him too much.

Today her walk is a holiday ramble, beloved of evangelical hikers, an adventure across the wild hills. For them the completion of that trek is an achievement to be celebrated.

For Mary it was nothing. It was what you did.

The grave of Thomas Charles, St. Bueno's Church Llandycil

Caio, Carmarthenshire
John Harries 1839

Unless the above amount is paid to me … adverse
means will be resorted to for the recovery

This is a grave that either contains mysteries – or contains nothing
at all.

The grave of John Harries, Caio

It is simple and unassuming, close to the wall of the parish church in Caio in Carmarthenshire. It is the grave of John Harries who, together with his son Henry, became known as one of the *dyn hysbys* (cunning men) of Cwrtycadno. They achieved considerable fame and notoriety in the early nineteenth century. And whilst the gifts they paraded were, allegedly, shared by many in the family, John (1785 – 1839) and Henry (1821-1849), were the most notable exponents of the dark arts.

The family lived at Cwrtycadno at Pantcoy in the Cothi valley and both John and Henry received a conventional education. They both went to Haverfordwest Grammar School. John trained as a surgeon, probably in Edinburgh. He then practised in Harley Street in London, interestingly with an astrologer called Robert Smith, also known as *Raphael*. Henry, his son, later attended London University and the Royal College of Surgeons.

When John returned to the Cothi valley, he used an unusual combination of conventional training and traditional remedies in his practice. Anxious people came from far and wide, to consult him on matters involving healing (both human and animal), fortune-telling and prophecy, much of the work undertaken with the aid of astrological projections.

These were superstitious times. Any sort of learning or knowledge had a mysterious quality. In a semi-literate society, book ownership was not very widespread. Most homes would contain only a Bible. However, John Harries had an extensive library, containing his medical books and various Latin and Greek texts. A library was dangerous, something to be feared, full of unknown things. And these things gave the Harries family huge power. Belief in witchcraft and magic was commonplace. Urban society might scoff and embrace all those scientific and technical advances that changed nineteenth century life with unbridled enthusiasm. Out in the country, however, the old beliefs persisted – and Caio, deep in the Cothi valley, was certainly remote.

The people who lived there believed in them because they wanted to, because they wanted simple answers to complex problems. They believed that Harries family could intercede for them and call down solutions from the supernatural world because they had wisdom; because they had power.

They were seen as charmers and healers, who could stop bleeding, heal wounds and cure skin disease, whilst restoring mental balance. If I am honest, I wouldn't mind an appointment myself, at my age. They promoted their ability to influence both the mind and the body of their patients and seemed to promote the use of fresh spring water as a cure for most things. Obviously, the concept of *For goodness sake pull yourself together* had its pernicious hold in rural Wales, even then.

The division between religion and superstition was blurred. Everyone went to church but accepted without question the concept of demonic possession and still believed in witchcraft. A man came to see Dr John because he was convinced that he was bewitched. He had had numerous treatments from other doctors with no effect. Harries abused the family for taking him to see *quack* doctors and said that obviously his problems had started when he swallowed an evil spirit in the shape of a tadpole, which had grown into a frog. He consulted his books and called upon the spirits which made the patient vomit – and yes, you are right, there amongst the vomit was a frog. As I understand it, such a thing still happens on a Saturday night in Cardiff, although the necessary research required to verify this is not an attractive prospect.

It was particularly the claims made that they could predict the future, recover missing property and consult with the supernatural, that brought father and son notoriety. Henry was never inclined to shy away from publicity. He promoted his ability to *determine what places best to travel in or reside in, trade or profession best to follow, and whether fortunate in speculation, viz lottery, dealing in foreign markets etc.* These are services which, sadly, my own general practice does not currently offer.

He claimed to be able to determine whether marriage would prove happy or otherwise, and whether children were born lucky or not, from *the planetary orbs at the time of birth*. Sadly, however, in this, Henry was unable to help himself.

He married Hannah Marsden in the face of some hostility from his family. He was felt to be marrying beneath him, for she was the daughter of a local workman in Caio, but he told everyone that he had no choice. Their union had been pre-ordained in their astrological charts. Sadly it was not a happy marriage. Perhaps he had missed that part in the stars.

It was also said that after John's death in 1839, Henry tried to contact *Raphael* to explore the possibility of communicating with his father in the spirit world- which, in fact, was far more difficult than he realised, since *Raphael* had died eight years earlier.

It cannot be a surprise that stories attached themselves to them, like barnacles. One of the most famous cases involved a local girl who had disappeared. Dr John was consulted and he immediately told the family that she had been murdered by her lover. He told them where the body was buried, near Maes yr On, under a tree with a bees nest, next to a stream. And, of course, they found her. Her lover confessed.

But the magistrates called Harries before them. Clearly he knew too much. Perhaps he was involved, so he was charged with aiding and abetting the murder. How else could he have known? His defence was a simple one, based upon his ability to predict the future. He promised the magistrates that if they would tell him the hour of their birth, *'I will tell you the hour you will die.'* They quickly set him free.

People would travel on long journeys to see John Harries, to discover the whereabouts of their lost cattle, for example. Once, after a fruitless search, a woman sought advice from him about her lost wedding ring. On her arrival, and before she could speak, Dr John told her that a relative would hand it over. On her return home, her son handed over the ring, and expressed both his regret at taking it and his relief that he could now die in peace, as he did two days later. Similar stories about him using his gifts to recover lost spoons perhaps suggest a certain wasting of talent.

But even such revelations were to be feared. An old man sought their help to recover money he had lost. Harries promised that he would certainly get his money back and that the thief would be punished by being bedridden. Good news for the old man, for revenge is always sweet. Except that the money had been taken by his wife. She took to her bed and remained there for 18 years.

The doctors were ready to generate their own mythology and projected an image of themselves they were happy to promote. They would conclude their bills with '*Unless the above amount is paid to me … adverse means will be resorted to for the recovery.*' Sceptics might say they '*gulled the credulous for many years and reaped a bountiful harvest,*' but for many, the Harries were not men who you would wish to have as enemies. They inspired fear and compliance.

And yet no matter how good the physician was, he could not grant himself immortality. Henry's health was delicate. He died of consumption in 1849, aged 28. As far as his father is concerned, it is said that Dr John had seen his own death written in the stars. It had apparently been booked in for 11 May 1839 and thus to avoid his fate, John took to his bed for the whole day. However, the house caught fire. He ran downstairs and went up a ladder to throw water on the roof. The ladder slipped and he fell and was killed.

His body was taken to Caio and, as the bearers approached the churchyard, the coffin suddenly became lighter. This was, they said, because the Devil had taken possession of his body, just as he had previously taken possession of his soul.

Obviously.

Cardiff
Albertina 1896

It is not every day that a lady parachutist is found in so terrible a predicament.

From earth to air to water and then finally back to earth.

Louisa Maud Evans rests in Cathays cemetery in Cardiff, beneath a white marble headstone.

Brave woman, yet in years a child
Dark death closed here thy heavenward flight.
God grant thee, pure and undefiled
To reach at last the light of light.

Louisa, 14 years old and working under the name of Albertina, was a parachutist who floated down from a trapeze suspended beneath a smoke-filled balloon. And a large crowd in Cardiff watched her die.

Louisa had run away from home. As far as we can know, she was born in Barton Regis in Bristol in late 1881. When she was 16 months old, she was adopted by a local photographer and painter called William Crinks and his wife Mary. She eventually went to work as a 'cloth factory girl,' but she clearly craved a life with rather more thrills. So, she ran away at the age of 14 to become a circus apprentice and a trapeze artiste. Soon *Mademoiselle Albertina* was working for *'Professor'* Auguste Eugene Gaudron.

He might have liked to call himself *'Professor,'* but he was a balloon manufacturer from Paris who had settled in London and who had become a significant figure in the world of ballooning. He once crossed the North Sea to Sweden in a balloon called *'Mammoth'* and he was the first balloonist to be issued with a passport when he flew non-stop to Russia. But he was also a showman who knew how to draw in the crowds and he did so, not just with his balloons, but with his parachutes.

Parachuting was already a century old and was strictly a circus stunt linked to the practise of smoke ballooning.

A fire pit was prepared, with a covered trench leading to the balloon. A blaze was built and then covered with wet straw to create hot smoke. This would then travel along the covered trench to fill a balloon, which was nothing more than a large cotton bag, tethered between posts. When it was full, *'the aeronaut'* would be buckled to a parachute that was attached to the balloon. If it was a young girl, then so much the better. She might even be seated on a trapeze.

Hot air always rises and so when the balloon was released it would ascend, perhaps to 2000 feet. Then the aeronaut would release the parachute and float back to earth.

There would be a weight, usually a sandbag, attached to the top of the balloon. When the weight of the aeronaut had gone, the balloon would naturally invert, the smoke would be released, and the balloon would fall to earth.

Of course, it was a show, nothing more. A pretty young girl, a sense of daring, a possibility of drama. It was dangerous, of course, which made the whole thing rather racy. And it wasn't science; it was merely a circus stunt.

The balloons themselves were not always well maintained. They could rip from over-heating or burn or the lines could tangle. But it required little in the way of equipment and showmen would tour the country, taking their wonder to small towns. But The Grand Exhibition in Cardiff had the potential to draw large crowds, full of excited young men, eager to watch a girl on a flying trapeze. This would be the ideal occasion for a showman.

Cardiff Central Library needed an extension and what better

way to pay for it than a Grand Exhibition of Industry and Fine Art in Cathays Park? There was a *'Grand Water Spectacle'* and open air opera with *'brilliant illumination of the grounds.'* There was even a model of a working dairy and a biscuit factory. It was, truly, full of thrills. In fact, when the Prince and Princess of Wales visited on 27 June 1896 it became the subject of the very first news item ever filmed in Britain. Louisa's performance on Tuesday 21 July 1896 at 7.30 pm was watched by crowds in the park. And all proceeded normally and calmly. The balloon ascended and then she descended slowly and steadily beneath her parachute. Except that the wind caught her and blew her out to sea.

It was that simple. Nothing complicated or dramatic. Just a gentle descent to death by drowning. *'Slowly, very slowly, did the lady descend and one could not but marvel how she managed to withstand the strain on her hands.'*

But once Albertina hit the water she disappeared.

She had ascended wearing, ironically, a nautical outfit – *'a nautical hat, a blouse and knickers'* She appeared *'cheery and confident.'* However, there was a breeze blowing from the north-west which took the balloon quickly into the sky, much higher than had been planned.

Gaudron claimed that he had told her to release herself over the Infirmary, but she didn't, and the balloon was carried swiftly over the Bristol Channel. This in itself was not enough to cause him alarm, since she was wearing a cork waistband as a lifebelt. He claimed that she was quite happy to come down in the open sea, which might suggest that she had done something like it before. It is believed that she had made three previous ascents in a balloon in Dublin before she came to Cardiff. However, whether she had used a parachute before is not clear. She released herself, the parachute opened and she floated gently down near the East Buoy.

For a while the parachute remained open and she was able to walk the water but after a few minutes she apparently disappeared.

Dockers watched her float over their heads at Roath. An engine driver put on steam and took his engine to the end of sidings to watch her come down. A fisherman called Partridge went out in a boat but couldn't find her. A local man called James Dunn, swam out towards the parachute but when he reached the spot it had vanished. Oh yes, Louisa's tragedy was a very public one. She was watched by the coastguards too, and it appeared to them that she had been picked up by a schooner, something which was to play a large part in the story over the next few days. A great deal of faith was placed in this mysterious vessel, for everyone wished fervently that she was safe. The press however was more realistic. *The Daily Post* expressed its reservations very elegantly.

Rumours of rescue are by the score but they are rumours and nothing more.

The paper goes on to say

It is not every day that a lady parachutist is found in so terrible a predicament.

On Wednesday we are told that Mr Tucker loaned his tug, *Cormorant,* to join the search party. Policemen were onboard with grappling irons and crowds watched from the shoreline as they dragged the seabed.

They found nothing, apart from the balloon stuck in the mud. The rumours said that she had been picked and put ashore at Clevedon or Clifton or perhaps Penzance. It was even suggested that it was all an elaborate publicity stunt. She would soon be revealed to general acclaim and business would boom.

Local fishermen though, shook their heads. If her ropes had become entangled, then the speed of the tide could have dragged her under the water. She would have been taken up to Newport. That was where they should look. They resumed dragging operations on Thursday.

In the absence of hard evidence, there was a flurry of speculation about the state of mind of the *fair aeronaut Albertina.*

31

Another performer at the Exhibition, a young man called Owen, said he had spoken to her earlier in the day. Albertina had been worried about something, he said; she had appeared nervous. He claimed that he tried to dissuade her from the performance but she replied *'I've got something on my mind and I am going up. I don't care if I come down alive or not.'* Before the ascent she seemed better and Owen offered to collect her by cab following her descent. He agreed to bring her a drink of milk as she requested and said goodbye. *'Tra-la-la'* she replied, and then the ascent began. She would never speak to anyone else again.

She was found on Friday night, without her parachute, her body washed up at the mouth of the Usk in Newport.

The recovery of the body is described in the press in an elegant piece of writing. *After being tossed in the eddying currents and races and shoals of the Severn Estuary, the bruised cork-belted Albertina cast up on wave-washed shingle, within sound of the harsh death-song of the clanging bell-buoy*

She was found by Mary Waggett, a girl of almost identical age, close to the lighthouse at Nash and so, in the early hours of Saturday morning, *'the corpse was raised from its couch of tidal mud.'*

Gaudron was criticised by the coroner for his lack of judgement in allowing the ascent to proceed but the verdict was death by drowning.

It was such a public death and the public who had watched her needed to recognise this terrible waste. They responded through a public subscription to pay for a funeral and for the expensive white marble headstone, whose words encapsulate the terrible sense of waste. Of course, Louisa was replaced. The show must go on, after all. Others followed. Others died too. One girl landed safely on a roof and then fell off. But they had to be girls. Gaudron understood the glamour and excitement that they brought to the performance. Not only that, they attracted young men who came to see the irresistible risk-taking beauties, doing something that seemed so daring and which they could not do themselves.

Gaudron's career as a showman and entertainer did not diminish. He worked with Buffalo Bill and his travelling circus for a while. Gaudron is buried in Highgate Cemetery in London in 1913 in a tomb topped by a stone balloon. Louisa is buried in Cardiff, where she came to earth.

She would be very difficult to find if it were not for the excellent Cathays Cemetery Heritage Trail which has helpfully marked some of the more notable graves in its extensive grounds. Louisa's is number 18. You should enter the cemetery from Allensbank Road and park on the curve where the path widens. Walk into the cemetery and bear left and you will find her just off the main path on the left hand side. Look for grave marker 18 in section G. And then remember that she was only 14.

Louisa Maud Evans in Cathays Cemetery, Cardiff

Chepstow Gwent
Henry Marten 1680

The man who killed the King.

The porch of St Mary's Church Chepstow, where Marten lies

The grave of Henry Marten is just inside the door of St. Mary's Church in Chepstow. As you walk in his grave stone is under your feet, hidden by a red carpet, as if his presence is an embarrassment. As it might well be, for this is a man who killed his king.

You can stand alongside the notices and the cards and the chest collecting donations for church funds and then, discreetly, you can roll back the red carpet. Underneath, you will find an inscription, unsurprisingly rather worn now, but you can work it out, with

34

patience.

'Here was buried a true Englishman, who in Berkshire was well known...'

And in Chepstow too, where he was a notable resident of its castle, for Marten was the man who turned that castle into a home.

In good seventeenth century tradition, his epitaph is a bit of a joke, an acrostic poem. The first letter of each line spells out his name. He probably enjoyed presenting it like this. It was clearly worked out a long time in advance, too, for death took him completely by surprise, at dinner. He probably wouldn't have minded too much. Henry Marten was always a man for enjoying himself.

Here or elsewhere, all's one to you, or me,
Earth, air or water gripes my ghostless dust,
None knows how soon to be by fire set free,
Reader, if you an oft tried rule will trust,
You'll gladly do and suffer what you must.
My life was spent with serving you and you,
And death's my pay, it seems, and welcome too,
Revenge destroying but itself, while I
To birds of prey leave my old cage and fly,
Examples preach to the eye; care then (mine says)
Not how you send but how you spend your days.

He had an eventful life and a dramatic one, for what he did put him, and others, beyond redemption. Yet Henry Marten got away with it. Everyone knew him; everyone had an opinion about him. He never hid himself away and was a survivor when he had no right to be.

Marten was certainly never Welsh, for he was an Englishman

through and through and played a huge part in one of the most significant events in our past. And yet he is buried in Wales. So I think we have a responsibility to remember the remarkable part that he played in history, because that is what brought him to us. Marten was a man who lived through the tumultuous times of the English Civil War, times that he graced with his forthright opinions and his free spirit, unmoved always by public opinion.

He was born in Oxford in 1602 and his father was a prosperous lawyer, providing his son with the prosperity upon which he could base the rest of his life. He certainly indulged himself. It was said that his company was *incomparable* but that he *would be drunk too soon.*

He was educated in University College, Oxford and entered Parliament as member for Berkshire. This was to be the arena where he created his little place in history, though it is said that he spent much of his time there asleep. When he was awake, he was outspoken and opinionated and was deeply in tune with the spirit of his times. It is ironic that one of his homes, the Rectory in Hinton Waldrest in Oxfordshire, is a beautiful English house, one that that speaks of wealth and privilege and centuries of history. Yet Marten did his very best to overturn the status quo that had created him. He was one of the first to call openly for the overthrow of the monarchy and was regarded as a leader for all manner of extremists.

His contemporaries regarded Marten as immoral and such was his reputation that he united all shades of opinion against him. Both the King and Cromwell separately described him as a *'whoremaster.'* Charles I once ordered him to leave a race meeting in Hyde Park because his presence was offensive. *'Let that ugly rascal be gone out of the park.'* His private life was certainly colourful. In an attempt to control a wild and promiscuous son, (*' a great lover of pretty women'*) his father arranged a marriage to Margaret Staunton, a rich widow. He even bought them a house in Shrivenham in Oxfordshire as a wedding present. Margaret moved in, but Henry didn't. He stayed in London with his mistress, Mary Ward, with whom he lived quite openly and had three daughters. Yet he was not altogether a neglectful husband, because Margaret apparently had at least seven children. At the end of his life they spent a happy and contented imprisonment together. But more of that later.

His relationship with Mary was celebrated in his letters to her that were published in 1662 under the title, *Henry Marten's Familiar Letters to his Lady of Delight*. It is a very nice title but its publication was probably an attempt to discredit him. It didn't work and he enjoyed the publicity, for Marten was a man without shame.

Neither was he a person to mince his words. In Parliament some of the things he said about the king were so extreme that Charles demanded his arrest and his trial for high treason. At one point, he spoke of preparing the king for heaven. In August 1643 he was even expelled from Parliament and imprisoned in the Tower of London by his colleagues, for saying that the destruction of one family was preferable to the destruction of many families. Marten had strong views about most things and was a man of little compromise. He was a zealous and committed republican and his beliefs were completely unshakable. He later had the King's statues pulled down and seized the royal regalia in Westminster Abbey, saying that *'there would be no further use of these toys and trifles.'* During the Civil War he was made governor of Aylesbury and he raised a regiment of troops in Berkshire, proclaiming that they fought *'for the people's freedom against all tyrants whatsoever.'* He obtained horses for them by stopping travellers on the highways. His regiment marched around the country seemingly at random, and independently of any Army command. In any circumstances, he always believed that he was completely right and questioned the sincerity of the views of his colleagues. He expressed considerable doubts about Oliver Cromwell, arguing that his ambition was effectively undermining the establishment of a true republic. Indeed, he claimed to be planning Cromwell's murder, with a pistol and dagger always ready for such a purpose. He seemed to believe that only he himself had kept the faith.

He acted together with Cromwell to bring Charles 1 to trial and helped to draft the charges against him. It was a key moment in European history and those involved seemed to recognise this. Marten and Cromwell had a fit of the giggles when it came to signing the death warrant and began to flick ink at each other, like guilty schoolboys. But like all the signatories, Marten had no second thoughts.

The King was executed because these men, the Regicides, believed it right and necessary. And it was done in broad daylight, with the full majesty of the law. Cromwell said, '*It was not a thing done in a corner.*' But there would be a price to pay - and a very heavy price - for those who signed that death warrant.

Marten worked to establish the Commonwealth which was so important to him. He was a member of the committees that supervised the abolition of the monarchy and the House of Lords and was granted land as a reward for his services in overthrowing the king. However, he could not manage the lands he was given with any success and found himself heavily in debt. He was forced into retirement from politics in 1653 and spent some time in prison again, this time for debt.

He was regarded as an atheist, but in fact he argued for toleration, showing equal contempt for most shades of religious opinion. As far as he was concerned, religious toleration should be extended to Roman Catholics, because they were just as wrong as any other faith.

On the Restoration of the monarchy, he made no attempt to escape and was tried for his part in the king's death. He was indeed sentenced to death by the Commons but spared by the House of Lords. So he escaped the death penalty, unlike many of the other regicides who were executed as an act of revenge. That may have been a recognition of the fact that he had protected Royalists in the 1650s. He certainly argued against the execution of the royalist poet Sir William Davenant on the grounds that he was too rotten

38

a rogue to be turned into a sacrifice. Oh yes. he was inconsistent but only because he was true to his own opinions.

The sentence was commuted to life imprisonment and he was imprisoned in Chepstow Castle. The part of the castle where he had rooms became known as Marten's Tower and he seems to have had a comfortable existence there, enjoying the freedom of the town. Margaret and he occupied one apartment and his servants had the one above. He received visitors and was himself a welcome guest at neighbouring mansions. In this untroubled style he lived for almost eighteen years. He died on 9 September 1680 having choked while eating his supper.

The worn grave of Henry Marten

Marten was a character, a significant figure in our history. He says on his tomb '*My life was spent with serving you and you,*' and that was fine, just as long as you agreed with him. Yet in the eighteenth century his grave was an embarrassment. His actions and the part he had played in executing his king were unforgivable. So his stone was moved from the chancel to his current location where he is now trodden, unseen, underfoot.

Cribyn, Ceredigion
The Murders of Mary Evans and her son Samuel 1919

A murder of a most revolting nature

You will find the Chapel opposite the old post office on the corner as you drive into the village of Cribyn from Lampeter. The compact graveyard at the rear is neat and well maintained. The gravestone you seek is still intact and easy to find and it might appear unexceptional to those who do not know. It remembers a father and mother joined in death, along with their son. John had died seventeen years earlier, aged 34. Mary was 47 and Samuel was 22 when they joined him. And then you will see that Mary and Samuel died on the same day, 29 April 1919. And that is because they died in *'a murder of a most revolting nature,'* a crime which remains unsolved.

The gravestone leans alarmingly to one side and before too long it will collapse. But it represents the story of a *'dark and dreadful deed'* which shocked the whole of west Wales. The most unnatural of crimes. A mother apparently murdered by one of her sons. But which one?

The family home was Clawddmoel Farm near Ffynonoer, just outside Temple Bar. The reporter for the *Cambrian News and Welsh Farmers Gazette* said *'Seldom have I seen a poorer abode. Half stone, half clay with corrugated iron sheets covering the defects of a thickly thatched roof.'* In fact, what he was looking at was quite a successful smallholding. It was *'no habitation for human beings'* he said. Perhaps he needed to get out more. There were places much worse than Clawddmoel Farm. Here in the countryside, five miles north west of Lampeter, it was perfectly acceptable.

Father, Mother, Son, Cribyn

In fact, Mary had done very well. She was 48 and had been widowed suddenly in 1902. Her husband John had never seen his fifth son, Willie. But now she owned Clawddmoel and had bought additional land. *'By dint of hard work and rigid economy,'* she had succeeded.

Perhaps it would help at this stage if we thought about Mary's five sons.

She had given birth to their first child before she married John, so effectively the eldest son, John Lewis Evans, was illegitimate. How much the other boys, especially James, knew of this isn't clear. In 1919 John was 24 and serving in the army in Egypt and, however supportive he was of his mother, had no legal status.

Samuel, 22, was the eldest legitimate son – *'a manly specimen…(who) made a soldierly figure in his uniform.'* He had been a prisoner of war in Germany for two years and had finally returned

42

home four months earlier.

James, who was 20, lived on the farm and had maintained it in the absence of his elder brothers, after previously working in the Pembrey Munitions works.

There was Thomas, who was 18 and a collier at Tycroes near Ammanford.

Finally, we have Willie, who had been born after his father's death, in May 1902. At the time of the murders, he was 16 and attended school in Aberaeron.

So five brothers. All apparently harmonious and supportive, but who could know the tensions which simmered within the home, the festering sores that were forever poked and prodded?

Tuesday 29 April 1919 was a busy morning. Everyone had things to do. Willie was off to Aberaeron at 9.00am for the start of the school term. Samuel had left in the cart to collect manure from Ystrad station at 10.00am. James said he was sent by his mother to Lampeter to check on the health of a relative at 10.30 am. He bought some shoelaces, spoke to a number of people and had a lift home in a cart.

We will never know for certain what happened. All we can say with any certainty is that Samuel was found by James at about 4.30 pm, with a gunshot wound to the back of his head, lying in the passage leading to the kitchen. In the kitchen he found his mother '*with her head splintered with gunshot.*' She had been shot from behind in the nape of the neck whilst knitting in front of the fire. '*An unfinished stocking with needles attached*' was on the floor. The fire was out, her body was cold. Significantly, when the murderer came in, she appeared to have shown no inclination to turn round. It was clear that she had been shot first and then Samuel, who had come to see what was going on. Nothing in the house appeared to have been taken, although later it was realised that Mary's purse was missing. Samuel still had over £15 in his pocket. The two farm guns were still in their rack but they had been used recently. When the doctor arrived he declared that they had died before noon.

Suicide was never an option. It was murder and the circumstantial evidence pointed in one direction only. After all, you are always likely to be murdered by someone who knows you. Mary owned the farm, she had money in the bank and insurance policies in a drawer – she was insured for £150 and her sons for £100 each. Given the illegitimacy of John and the death of Sam, James would inherit. But it seems that he had previously been told by his mother that he would have to go to sea to work as a sailor in order to make way for his brother Sam.

How unhappy was James? At twenty six acres the farm was too small to keep two men. Mary, a domineering personality, had decided that Sam, liberated at last and now the returning war hero and the centre of attention, was the one who would stay. James, who had been working the farm, now would have to relinquish his position and go to sea. Is this really what he wanted?

On Monday, James bought twenty five cartridges and collected a family gun from a neighbour who'd previously borrowed it. The police found nineteen cartridges in a box in the parlour. There were others elsewhere in the house too.

James and Willie were quickly arrested. Did this indicate that the police didn't know what else to do? Or the fact that the Chief Constable had received a pay rise, prominently announced in the papers on the same day as the news of the murders, which he thus needed to justify by presenting himself as a man of decision? Certainly, as the defence counsel said, there was not enough evidence to hang a dog. All the police ever had was circumstance. They could not prove that either of the sons was at home at the right time to commit a double murder.

The prosecution had a motive, but they couldn't pin it on one brother exclusively. James seemed to have a cast-iron alibi. It was almost as if he went out of his way to be noticed in Lampeter on that day.

Willie's story was more troubling. He had been the first to leave to catch an early train to Aberaeron, carrying his heavy bags and some butter for his landlady. But he didn't go straight to the station. He said that his mother had sent him to a neighbouring farm to check whether they had started potato planting, so that she could go and help. But evidence in court suggested that she'd had an answer to that question the day before. And if he was going back with a message for her, why did he take his bags with him in the first place? Was it adolescent cunning? Or adolescent stupidity?

In fact, there were about two hours he couldn't properly account for. Willie said he had been lying down in a field for a while, for reasons he could not explain. The only time he was seen was when he appeared in a shop at Temple Bar, just before noon, to buy cigarettes. He eventually caught the train to Aberaeron just after midday, went to his lodgings and then went out and bought a bicycle with eleven £1 notes. Willie said his mother had given him the money – from her purse which had gone missing. He told the shopkeeper that he wanted to take the bike home to show his mother, but in fact he just cycled round Aberaeron in an excited way for the rest of the evening. Why? In July a boy who was lodging in the same house would find six £1 notes hidden in Willie Evans' algebra book. Where had they come from? Oh no, Willie's story wasn't convincing at all.

The case came to court in November 1919. There had been significant shortcomings in the investigation. Items been moved so no one could be sure whether breakfast had been cleared away or lunch prepared; the guns hanging on the wall had been handled so there was no hope of fingerprints; the bodies had been moved; there was no examination of stomach contents, so had they eaten dinner or not? James, the accused, had spent the night in the house after the murder.

They had absolutely no hope of establishing even an approximate time for the murders and that was always the key. Who was where, and at what time?

The police could only ever prove where the victims had been found, since they were lying dead on the floor. The only witnesses to what happened at breakfast were the two who the police had arrested. What if Sam had been back before James left? What if Willie did indeed go home?

The judge said that the defence offered by either boy was free from doubt, but there was simply no convincing evidence to support a conviction. So James and Willie were acquitted.

It is a remarkable story, a fading tragedy represented by a shifting gravestone. A story of sibling rivalry, avarice, murder? Possibly. But now you have read this, ask yourself one question. Did Willie Evans really kill his mother so that he could have a bicycle?

Hendre, Gwent
Charles Rolls 1910

The Man Who Fell to Earth

It is a long way down the hill to the stunningly beautiful church of St. Cadoc, just behind the impressive family home, Hendre, the 'winter dwelling.' A gentle, prosperous place, timeless and untroubled. Enter the church yard and look up the hill to the left and you will see three Celtic crosses. Some of the graves here are showing signs of wear but not these three. Mother, father and their son. And when you go up to face them, the one on the right marks the grave of one of the most famous names in British Engineering. Charles Stuart Rolls.

Charles Rolls in the Church of St Cadoc

47

There is also a statue of him in the centre of Monmouth, overlooking the traffic, in front of the statue of Henry V. He stands in the middle of all the bustle, holding an aeroplane, for flying was his last and greatest love. It is also what killed him.

He was born into money and privilege, in Berkeley Square in London in August 1877. He was the third son and as such was not set for inheritance. He had to find his own way. And he did. He became a household name, personifying daring, excitement and excellence.

There are those who speculate that his future partner, Frederick Royce, actually delivered birth congratulations telegrams to the family, since he was working as a post office messenger at the time, but there is no evidence to suggest that this happened. But there can certainly be no doubt that Charles had money. His father, John Rolls, was a justice of the Peace and High Sherriff of Monmouthshire. Later he became Baron Llangattock of the Hendre.

Like so many boys from such a privileged background, Charles went to school in Eton. His interest in technology and engineering was present from an early age. In fact, before he went up to Trinity College in Cambridge, he installed a dynamo at Hendre and wired part of the house. He loved boy-things, gadgets and toys. And in October 1896, one of the most important events in his life took place when he went to Paris. With his father's help he bought a Peugeot Phaeton, the first car ever seen in Cambridge, they say. As a result, he became known as *'Petrolls'*, because, typically perhaps, he couldn't leave his new toy alone. This enthusiasm was to shape his destiny. In fact, as a student he joined with others across the country to break the law that restricted cars to 4 mph. As a result of this defiance, the limit was increased to 12 mph. After his graduation in 1898, he worked in the railway workshops at Crewe but his main passion remained cars. He began importing French vehicles, and in one of them, in 1903, he established a world land speed record of 93 mph in Dublin. His company began in Fulham, but soon had showrooms in Mayfair. He was described as an *'automobilist'* and his adventures in these early days included driving overnight from London to Cambridge and then from Knightsbridge to The Hendre in time for Christmas. A day trip for us on motorways. An adventure on coach roads back then.

It was the following year, in the Midland Hotel in Manchester in 1904, that he was introduced to Frederick Royce. This was a significant and life-changing moment. Royce had been Chief Electrical Engineer responsible for a street lighting scheme in Liverpool and had started his own business selling electric cranes and dynamos. But he was looking for a means of expansion into the developing motor industry. He also started with French cars, making adaptations and modifications and was soon making his own. Legend tells us that on his return to London, Charles told his business partner, *'I have found the greatest motor engineer in the world.'* He agreed to take the whole car output of Royce Limited, which would then be sold exclusively by Rolls, under the name of Rolls Royce. These two men had so little in common. Their backgrounds and their abilities were entirely different and yet they became partners and good friends. Their reputation was soon established as the manufacturers of high quality cars.

Charles Rolls successes in various motoring competitions promoted the reputation of their cars. The 1907 Scottish Reliability Trial involved driving 15,000 miles, after which any worn parts were replaced. The Silver Ghost won with necessary replacements cost just over £2. As a result, the motoring press described it as *'the best car in the world'* and the reputation of Rolls Royce was sealed.

However, Charles' sense of adventure was taking in a new direction. He became very interested in ballooning and then in powered flight. He established links with the Wright Brothers and, when he went to Le Mans to meet them in 1908, he was taken up in a plane for the first time. He was hooked. He devoted his time to aviation and was the second person to be awarded a pilot's licence by the Aero Club in March 1910. His greatest flight was a few months later on 2 June 1910, when he made the first flight from England to France and back again, non-stop across the English Channel. He was a national hero, for these things were important in those times. He '*electrified the entire kingdom*' by his exploits, so the papers said. But six weeks later he was dead.

The newspaper headlines summed it up perfectly. *Daring Aviator Dashed to Death.*

Hon. Chas. Rolls Instantly Killed at Bournemouth in the presence of Spectators.

It was a flying tournament. The competition? Who could land their plane nearest to a given mark, which was right in front of the grandstand. He was flying a Wright's bi-plane which had been modified without authorisation. The tail piece snapped off and the framework crumpled. It fell from about 100 feet in the sky and shattered completely on impact. When they eventually dragged him from the tangled wreckage, they found that Charles had fractured his skull. Such was his fame that speeches were interrupted in the House of Lords to announce his death. The press indicates that he is the twelfth victim of the '*Science of Aviation*'. He was also the first Briton to die in an air accident. Unfortunate claims to fame that no one would have welcomed. The link between Rolls Royce and the aeronautics industry that has always flourished was created by Charles Rolls. His aristocratic, sporting enthusiasm helped to shape the future of the company and established the importance of the industry. His achievements were immense. In his short life, Charles Rolls gave a tremendous boost to both motoring and aviation. Furthermore, he contributed significantly to the belief that the Government needed to invest in the aeroplane technology in order to guarantee national security. He could see the possibilities as early as anyone else.

This is one of the graves that we have found that truly

represents a lovely day out. It is in a wonderful location. It is ironic, but it is only the recognition of a death that will take you out into the life-enhancing beauty of this lovely place. Leave Monmouth on the B4233 to Rockfield and then follow the B4347 towards the village of Newcastle. It is an unspoiled part of the country, peaceful and green and these are narrow quiet lanes. About two miles out of Rockfield there is, on the left of the road, a simple wooden signpost indicating 'Church'. Park here carefully, for the road is narrow, and then walk down the path, past the house and down to the sheltered church. The link between house and church is clear. There is a little white gate in the wall, through which the family would walk down easily from Hendre to the services, past the place where they now rest. The views here are beautiful and the church has a long and distinguished history. It is hard to imagine that in this isolated spot you will find the grave of a pioneer, a man famous throughout the world. The constant peace of this house must have been a huge contrast with the noise and excitement of the aeroplanes that he flew. He died too young, of course. There were so many other things that he wanted to do. There is real sadness in this too-early death, but his place in history is assured. Inside the porch of the church there is a stone in memory of John Powell, who died in 1816, aged 73. And the words on the stone are highly appropriate.

Praises on tombs
Are trifles vainly spent.
A man's good name
Is his own monument.

Charles' tomb has a simple inscription. *Blessed are the pure in heart for they shall see God.* And Charles was pure. Pure and faithful to his spirit of adventure. And his name, forever associated with the very best of British engineering, has indeed been his most significant monument.

Llanallgo. Anglesey
Stephen Roose Hughes 1862

Surrounded by eyes that could not see him

Moelfre is a beautiful village, in a sheltered bay. It has a long history of over 4000 years, beginning with an ancient burial chamber, And yet the central event, the one that still lives in the memory of Moelfre, is the wreck of *The Royal Charter,* when tumultuous seas offered it an unwanted place in history. Here you will find the notable lifeboat station, a neat and cheerful place. Exactly one hundred years to the day after the loss of *The Royal Charter,* they put to sea to rescue the crew of *The Hindlea.* It hit the same rocks – now called *'The Royal Charter Rocks'* - but this time all were saved.

They could do nothing in 1859. It was impossible to launch lifeboats anywhere on the west coast of Wales, for this was the *'Royal Charter Storm.'* The fiercest in living memory, a hurricane, later estimated to have reached Storm Force Twelve. One hundred and thirty three ships were wrecked, ninety were badly damaged. The South Devon Railway track was ripped up. Llandudno's hoped-for future as a terminal port for Irish sea-traffic disappeared when the new pier was turned to matchwood by the storm. In conditions of such ferocity, all ships were entirely alone.

No one and nothing on the west coast was safe. At Cwm yr Eglwys, in north Pembrokeshire, you can see all that remains of the twelfth century church of St Brynach. The rest was dashed away in the hurricane. The coffins of the vicar's six dead children were exposed and then washed out to sea. A hurricane doesn't care for much at all.

St Brynach's in Cwm yr Eglwys, Pembrokeshire, destroyed in the Royal Charter Storm

When Charles Dickens arrived to view the scene in Moelfre at the end of December 1859, everything was calm. The sea was placid and he watched divers continuing to recover gold from the wreck, divers who had spent Christmas there on the rocky beach, with roast beef and rum. In the days after the disaster, sovereigns had been scattered over the beach like seashells, but they had long since been collected.

It was quiet when we were there, too. There was a couple playing with their dog on the pebble beach below the holiday caravans, positioned carefully for the splendid view. This wasn't what Dickens saw. He saw *'masses of iron, twisted by the fury of the sea into the strangest forms'*. He comments that no more bodies had come ashore since last night. The expectation was that the spring tides would dislodge others still trapped in the wreckage. Although the wreck was only 25 yards from the shore, it took months for the bodies to come ashore. There were so many of them. Perhaps 450. It proved to be a grim harvest from an angry sea.

Dickens had come to see the Rector of St Gallgo's church in Llanallgo, at the top of the hill above Moelfre. Stephen Roose Hughes, like himself a prodigious writer, was a man who opened his house and his heart to distressed strangers. He was a true and unaffected Christian, *'delightfully genuine,'* with *'noble modesty.'* What he had done, with the help of his wife and of his brother, another clergyman called Hugh Robert Hughes, was worthy of recognition. That is why Charles Dickens travelled from London, quite unsolicited, to stay at the Panton Arms in Pentraeth and to offer his respect, for Stephen Roose Hughes became one of the heroes of the Royal Charter, although he was never on board.

The church of St. Gallgo is one of the oldest Christian sites in Anglesey and it had to accommodate one of the great sea disasters of the nineteenth century. Hughes converted it into a mortuary, where he worked *'surrounded by eyes that could not see him,'* amongst dead strangers who someone else had loved. And in the end, he also became one of its victims.

You can read Charles Dickens' gesture of respect for Hughes in his collection, *The Uncommercial Traveller*. The writing is clear and elegant, full of a genuine admiration for the man and what he did. Dickens read some of the many letters he received, what he describes as '*a shipwreck of papers.*' He tells us how Hughes examined ripped clothes and buttons, how he looked for distinguishing scars, crooked toes, tattoos. And all the time he was wrapped in the suffering and pain of others, seeking those who had been lost so suddenly, and offering their families support and compassion.

Their graves are scattered all over the north side of Anglesey, wherever the bodies washed ashore. They make the story of the shipwreck so horribly real. For example, in Llanallgo there is the small stone for William Thomson from Cardross in Dumbartonshire, who was an engineer in Hobart, Tasmania.

The grave of William Thomson, Llanallgo

There is a large chest tomb containing most of a family – James Davies and Louisa Francis and four of their children – twin daughters Sophie and Florence and their sons Walter and

55

Derwent. It was erected by their two surviving children. And this awful tragedy is still alive. The descendants of Marius Boyle, a miner who was lost, laid a memorial outside the door of the church for him in 2004.

At least they are named. In St Mary's Church in Pentraeth, there are stones paid for by Lady Vivien from Plas Gwyn. There are six small graves planted in a square. In the middle there is a larger stone erected in 1876. It says '*Near this stone lie buried six bodies which were washed ashore in this parish. They shall be mine saith the Lord of Hosts in that day when I make up my jewels.*' When you see these things, the tragedy becomes very real. Bodies, known and unknown that were once people just like you and me, were spoiled by sea and rocks.

Near this stone lie buried six bodies. Pentraeth

The ship was built in the Sandycroft shipbuilding yard near Chester for the Australian Steam Navigation Company. The launch in July 1855 inspired great interest, '*on account of its vast proportions and the novelty of the construction of such a ship on the banks of the Dee'.* It was a steam clipper, a hybrid ship, built of steel, a sailing vessel but one with the addition of a steam-driven propeller, installed to keep the ship moving in calm conditions.

On 26 August 1859 she left Melbourne for the last time. There were about 371 passengers and a crew of 112, though really, no one could be absolutely sure. There was plenty of official precious metals on board. There was a consignment in the cargo - Captain Taylor signed a receipt for £322,440 of gold. But the passengers had plenty of their own, for many of them were miners from the gold mines, returning home with their carefully accumulated and undeclared personal fortunes. Thus the true wealth on board can never be accurately calculated.

It was a tough voyage, with bad weather throughout. Ice bergs approached rather too close for comfort off Cape Horn, but the ship performed admirably and made excellent time. *The Northern Times* tells us that *'the greatest happiness prevailed amongst the passengers,'* and, in an act of some irony, *'off Ireland a collection was made for a testimonial to Captain Taylor and a purse made by the lady passengers for Rev Mr Hodge of New Zealand, who had discharged the religious duties during the voyage.'* In spite of the difficulties, this was a record-breaking run. Only 55 days to Ireland.

Then the barometer started to fall dramatically on 25 October. The Captain did consider putting into Holyhead harbour, as Brunel's *SS Great Eastern* had already done, but he felt he could outrun the approaching storm and maintain the ship's reputation for speed and an excellent service. It was 1.30 pm.

There are rumours that Captain Taylor was concerned to get back to Liverpool to break the record and to settle a wager and that his slippers were already warming by the fireside in a public house, but there is no evidence for these stories. The poor man was unlucky, that's all. He made an error of judgement and was caught out. But it was an error of judgement that killed.

Off Bardsey Island, the steam tug *United Kingdom* came alongside and asked if *The Royal Charter* would give a lift to eleven riggers on their way back to Liverpool. Such cruel luck. They boarded a ship heading for disaster.

Taylor signalled for a pilot to guide him into Liverpool from Point Lynas near Amlwch, but a pilot could not come out in such conditions. The winds reached hurricane force and swung around from east to north east, driving the ship inexorably towards Anglesey. They tried to fight the sea with their steam engines, but they were powerless. At 11.00 pm Taylor dropped anchor, but within 2 hours one anchor chains snapped and then the second. The crew frantically chopped down the masts to reduce the drag of the wind, but it made little difference. Then the propellers stopped, possibly fouled by the abandoned rigging. As a result, the crippled ship drifted on to a sandbank. The crew fired rockets and distress flares, but the storm was so fierce that those on the shore could do nothing other than watch. Lifeboats were lowered, but were instantly smashed by the waves.

On the ship things were grim indeed. The Captain tried to reassure passengers that they were safe from harm, now that they were on a sandbank. They were so close to the shore, perhaps twenty five yards; they were certain to be rescued. But in the conditions, they may as well have been twenty five miles from land. He quietly sent one of the crew to smash all the bottles of drink in the stateroom, to stop the crew drinking them. Whatever he may have said to the passengers, he knew things were desperate, One of the few survivors described the scene. *'Families were all clinging to each other; children were crying out piteously.'* The Reverend Hodge held a prayer meeting.

At this moment, a crew member offered to swim to the shore in the boiling sea with a line. Perhaps all disasters need a hero and the hero of that terrible night was called Joseph Rogers, although his real name was Giuseppi Ruggier, a Maltese seaman. His act of heroism was recorded by the artist Henry O'Neil in 1860, in a

58

painting called *A Volunteer.* Although badly injured by the waves that crashed him into the rocks, he managed to take a line to the shore. As a result, thirty nine men were saved. Women, however, were reluctant to trust their lives to the bosun's chair they had rigged up, so crew members used it and joined in the rescue from the shore. But no women or children were ever saved, though two boys aged 11 and 9 may have been washed ashore at Conwy, strapped to a plank and launched by their father.

Then a few moments before 7.00 am on 26 October 1859, the rising tide picked up the ship and drove her onto the rocks just to the north of Moelfre. Winds of over 100 mph then broke the ship in half. Passengers were *'closed up in the jaws of death.'* They fell into the sea along with machinery and ironwork. In these conditions, they had no hope at all. At the bow the crew might still be desperately operating the bosun's chair, but at the stern the passengers could only watch, separated from this fragile line to safety. Very quickly, both sections were destroyed by the immense power of the waves. Iron work eventually recovered from the wreck had sovereigns, and in one case a gold bar, driven into it as if it was nothing more substantial than clay.

No one really knows how many died, or indeed how much wealth the ship was carrying, for the Purser and his records were lost. It is believed that at least 450 died so close to the shore, and that many of those were dragged to the bottom by their money belts stuffed with gold, before being lifted up and beaten to death on the rocks. *'A gentleman named Welsh whilst in the lower saloon, tied two black canvas bags full of gold around his neck: he was lost.'* A man who did survive was Mr Taylor. He jumped into the sea with £35 and staggered to the shore with only 10 shillings and with most of his clothes ripped to shreds.

Captain Taylor *'succumbed to a sailor's fate.'* He was seen struggling in the water until a boat fell, hitting him on the head. He wasn't seen again.

The men of Moelfre, '*scattered quarrymen and fishermen*,' according to Dickens, formed a human chain and reached out into the waves to rescue who they could. They became known as '*The Twenty Eight*,' but there was little they could do. It had been sudden and it had been shocking and then it was over. The villagers provided warmth and shelter to the survivors as the storm abated, whilst the shoreline was suddenly covered in gold – and in bodies.

The ship had sailed 16,000 miles and was wrecked such a short distance from home and so close to the shore. The enormity and the speed of the disaster were hard to grasp.

It was reported by the steamer *Druid*, which arrived in Liverpool from Anglesey, having seen out the storm, that the wreck was being plundered and that the military had been dispatched to protect property. But there were also conflicting reports that everything found had been handed in to the Customs House agents, who kept a record of it all. The truth probably lies somewhere between. One reporter says '*I saw men picking sovereigns out of the holes of the rocks as if they were shellfish.*' You can't really blame them. There is a long tradition of harvesting what you can from the sea. The militia from Beaumaris and an Army detachment from Chester arrived to protect the gold and probably the greatest part was recovered. But there have always been rumours of families made rich by the gold they collected from the shore that day, or looted from the wreck. Yes, soldiers may have been sent to protect the site. But local knowledge is always crucial. Some was sure to have got away. And some scraps are sure to be there still. The wreck is still visited by divers, who are convinced by the seductive prospect of treasure. It might lie in shallow water, where visibility is very poor, but hope springs eternal.

You can see a piece of *The Royal Charter's* iron hull at the Seawatch centre at Moelfre and there is a memorial, erected in 1935, above the rocks where the ship was smashed, on the beautiful Anglesey coastal path. You can stand by it and look down at the quiet sea, as we did, beneath which the wreck still lies. Still visited by divers, who talk like fishermen, of the big one that got away, of gold that appears and then slips away again in the tide. It is the skeleton of bulkheads and ribs that never changes and it surrendered its dead slowly. Bodies were washed up on the beaches of Anglesey for weeks afterwards. Dealing with them was a mammoth task.

Roose Hughes realised that something needed to be done, and something that preserved dignity and humanity in the aftermath of this shocking tragedy. So he took the lead. The people were paid ten shillings for each body they brought up the steep track to the church of St Gallgo. In truth, it was not a great deal for such awful work. The bodies were laid out in the church, which became a mortuary. The furniture was removed and services held in the Church school, which later also held the inquests.

Many turned up to find bodies of their loved ones. The visitors would speak to the Rector and offer some details. Then Roose Hughes and his wife would search the long rows of bodies. If they felt they had a positive identification, they would take the relatives in to the church blindfolded, to save them from the full horror of the scene. They would allow them only to see one particular body.

Many more wrote letters. Roose Hughes replied to every one of them. Yet sometimes there was little to say. Bodies were often battered beyond possible identification. Many had dressed in haste and were not wearing their own clothes. Sailors could sometimes be identified by their tattoos, but it was harder with passengers. The presence of a receipt for the purchase of a parrot, for example, about which the family had heard in a letter, was not always sufficient. Many parrots went down with the ship. But Roose Hughes did what he could, checking and listing possessions, and noting distinguishing features.

One hundred and forty five bodies were buried in the small churchyard in graves of four, and then exhumed and reburied when identification was possible. Sometimes Roose Hughes performed a funeral service twice over the same body. He saw all this as his duty.

He replied to every letter he received, offering comfort and understanding. He wrote, in total, 1,075 letters. It was this remarkable compassion that drew Dickens to the church of St Gallgo.

Roose Hughes could not shake off the enormity of what he had to deal with. The effects on him were considerable. Dickens noted that he was *'unable for a time to eat or drink more than a little coffee now and then, and a piece of bread.'* He absorbed grief and pain and yearning and, by so doing, exhausted himself. It says as much on his grave.

His noble and disinterested exertions on the memorable occasion of the terrible wreck of The Royal Charter are well known throughout the world. The subsequent effects of those exertions proved too much for his constitution and suddenly brought him to an early grave.

Today his church is neat and comfortable, recently restored after a serious fire but, when we were there. his memorial obelisk was collapsing. It was originally raised by public subscription and placed in the church, but was moved outside in the early 20th century. The ground on which it stands is unstable and the obelisk leans and sags.

His own grave in the churchyard was once neglected and fell into disrepair, but it now receives proper attention. It was erected by his widow, Jane Anne, in memory of her loving husband brought to an early grave by the sense of duty that consumed him. The grave is enclosed behind railings and is easy to find. It is a proper memorial to a hero. He died on 4 February 1862. He was 47.

The grave of Stephen Roose Hughes, Llanallgo

Llandawke, Carmarthenshire
The Murder of Rebecca Uphill 1850

The Unquiet Graves of Laugharne

It all started when they decided to exhume the pig, but we shall come to that in a moment.

This story takes us back in time to Brixton Farm near Laugharne in Carmarthenshire in 1850. The farm is still there, a grade 2 listed building, and in 1850 the tenants were Thomas and Mary Ann Severne, who managed a busy farm with a small clutch of domestic servants. One of them was Rebecca Uphill and she is buried in the beautifully remote church of St Odoceus in Llandawke, at the top of the narrow lanes above Laugharne . Her grave represents this remarkable story, standing alone in the grass and displaying this inscription.

O ponder well her sudden fall,
Ye thoughtless blooming virgins all.
Ye little think who read this stone
How soon the case might be your own.

What does that mean? The *'case'* is clearly a reference to a coffin. Don't forget your mortality? Or perhaps it means, Beware! You may be poisoned.

On Sunday 1 September 1850 Rebecca Uphill, a servant at Brixton Farm, was *'convulsed by violent purging and vomiting'* and died in agony on the following Tuesday. The doctor decided that it was *'English cholera,'* and so she was buried hastily in the graveyard of Llandawke Church on Friday. However, another servant, Ann Beynon, had also been afflicted but survived, and in the following ten days there was growing concern about Rebecca's death. The two servants had eaten the same broth, the remains of which were given to the pigs, including the healthy old sow who had then promptly died in her sty. When the sow was eventually exhumed, according to the butcher, her liver showed signs of poisoning.

So Rebecca herself was then exhumed and her body examined on the altar of the church at Llandawke, after which her parts were dispatched for analysis. '*We are given to understand,*' said the press, '*that the body of the unfortunate young woman has shown such rapid symptoms of decomposition as to excite the suspicions of her relatives and neighbours.*'

Rebecca Uphill in Llandawke

Consequently, another death in the household was re-examined - that of the mistress of the farm, Mary Ann Severne - who had passed away nine weeks previously in July. So they dug her up too, from her grave in Laugharne churchyard and her viscera was delivered, in a jar within a pig's bladder, to the analyst Mr Herapath in Bristol, who confirmed that she had been poisoned with arsenic.

Mary, 30 years old, had been in delicate health for a while, suffering from '*bilious attacks*.' She could never have been described as robust; eating had always been a problem for her. On 21 July 1850 she was ill in bed, only picking at the rabbit broth that the cook, Betsy Gibbs, had made for her. Mary was not well enough to go to church on that Sunday morning, so her husband Thomas went on his own and saw some of the domestic staff there, including Rebecca, the house maid. It was her job to care for Mary, but Betsy the cook had insisted on staying behind at the farm, alone, to look after her.

After church, Thomas found that Mary's condition had deteriorated dramatically. She was producing yellow vomit and was very busy on the commode. Her face seemed blue and she complained that she could not see. The poor woman died later that evening. Given her previous illnesses, it was assumed that she had died of natural causes. But of course, after Rebecca died, they realised she had been poisoned.

Suspicion naturally fell upon Betsy Gibbs. At the inquest into Rebecca's death, Ann Beynon said that she had felt the broth burn her throat. She had asked Betsy about it, who blamed the pepper she had sprinkled on a stale mutton chop she'd added. When the remains were put out for the sow, there was a noticeable white deposit on the base of the saucepan, which Betsy said was oatmeal. Both Rebecca and Ann were violently and repeatedly sick and, of course, the pig died. Betsy herself said, rather lamely, that she had been sick too, early in the morning, but no one else in the house was inclined to believe her. Suddenly the other employees on the farm refused to eat anything Betsy prepared for them.

The inquest was unanimous. After deliberating for fifteen minutes the jury returned a verdict of wilful murder against Betsy and she was taken to Carmarthen prison to await trial. She denied everything and kept on doing so.

What seems to have happened is that Betsy had ingratiated herself with her mistress to the extent that Mary asked her to be her husband's second wife. She didn't expect to live for very long, apparently. Betsy had already indicated to the other servants which of Mary's dresses she would wear for the wedding. The obvious conclusion, for some, was that she might have decided to help the sickly woman on her way.

But events ran out of control. Once Thomas' sister-in-law, Mrs Severne of Craigyburion, took over domestic management for him after Mary's death, and heard of Betsy's ambitions, she decided that she must be dismissed, to be replaced by Rebecca Uphill's sister, Jane Evans. That was when Rebecca was murdered.

Whilst held in prison on remand, Betsy confessed to the prison governor's domestic servant that she had given Mary arsenic in her camomile tea. When she came to trial in March 1851 there were other stories about her, too. She was wilful, argumentative, insolent and presumptuous. Betsy described Rebecca as a '*devil*' who would '*make me leave my place.*' She said that the decision to dismiss her made her '*angry in my heart. There will be somebody dead in a short time.*' She said that Ann and Rebecca should '*go from Brixton in the same way as my mistress did.*' She wanted to take a knife and '*rip open Ann's guts.*'

She tried to deflect attention away from her actions by talking about seeing corpse candles going from the door of the house and down the road, indicating the imminent route of a coffin. She claimed she could predict death, then suggested that she was possessed. '*The devil is here every night, putting me to sleep.*'

When the case went to the assizes in March 1851 it seemed that Betsy was doomed. But she was found not guilty, and for one very simple reason – the lack of conclusive evidence. The prosecution were unable to prove that Betsy had access to arsenic. Thomas Severne confirmed that there was some on the farm but no one knew where it was. Perhaps it had been wrongly labelled. They couldn't find anyone in the area who remembered selling arsenic to Betsy.

Margaret Lewis, a local woman known to everyone as Benny the Blacksmith's Widow, sometimes worked on the farm doing odd jobs. She was questioned, but denied ever buying arsenic, anywhere, for anyone. The chemist's wife in Laugharne, however, was sure that she had bought some from her.

Everyone suspected that Billy the Blacksmith's Widow had bought it for Betsy, on the pretence of dealing with a rat infestation in her cottage. But it could not be proved and Betsy was released.

Laugharne, however, did not believe she was innocent. It was said that she was attacked by a cow in the street that tried to gore her, which was seen as God's indication that she was guilty. An angry mob gathered outside her home and a trial was held. An effigy of Betsy was paraded through the streets, hanged from some gallows and then burnt as a witch. The next evening a mock funeral procession paraded along the street which they renamed 'Scape-the-Gallows-Street.' Shopkeepers refused to deal with her family. Eventually Betsy left Laugharne to live with her sister in Merthyr and Thomas Severne gave up his tenancy of the farm and moved away.

But the story wasn't over. There was an unexpected epilogue. Perhaps you will remember Jane Evans, Rebecca Uphill's sister, who was in line to succeed Betsy as cook? She was a widow, about 30 years old, with two children by her first husband. She was engaged to be married to Thomas Evans, who was 19, and by whom she was pregnant. Thomas was ready to marry her and adopt her children. The banns were published, despite opposition from his family, who felt he was much too young to take on such responsibility, but he could not be dissuaded.

Sadly, Jane died suddenly, a week after Betsy's acquittal. The greatest fear, of course, was that she too had been poisoned, perhaps by those hostile to her marriage. But there was no evidence. They decided she had a seizure, which the inquest interpreted as *Death by the Visitation of God*.

What happened to Jane's children is not known.

Llandudno

Walter Beaumont 1924

Walter – The Man-Fish

When we arrived in Llandudno we initially ignored the thrills of the excellent tramway; we did that in the afternoon. In the morning we went up the Great Orme by car, because we were looking for a grave. It is what we do. We went to the graveyard of St Tudno's Church, in its spectacular but rather exposed location, high above the sea, looking out towards the Lancashire coast. It took a while, but we found where Walter Beaumont is remembered, up in the top corner next to the boundary wall.

It is small and unassuming, a neat panel mounted on a piece of rough stone.

Professor Walter Beaumont. Died August 1924. Aged 69 years. Natus es Natandum Mortem ex undis rapuisti.

It means *'Born to swim - Death snatched from the waves.'* - a fine epitaph for a life-saver.

Walter was born in London in 1855 and showed an early proficiency in swimming. At the age of ten he rescued two brothers who fell into a canal and, in so doing, found his vocation. He first went to work in the merchant navy as a ship's engineer but appears to have spent much of his time keeping the unfortunate afloat in the oceans of the world. Not all of us find out what we are good at, but he was lucky. He did.

By 1880 he had become a professional swimmer and, in addition to working as a lifeguard in Llandudno, he developed a career as an entertainer, touring the world with his own troupe of female swimmers, which included his own daughter, Alice. Like manic goldfish, they provided thrills and spills inside a glorified fish tank.

The lucky residents of Rockhampton in Australia were thrilled, in October 1892, by the crystal glass tank, *'heated and illuminated,'* in which Walter – *'The Man-Fish'* - sat at the bottom and played a game of cards whilst smoking a cigar.

'The cards over, Lily Vane, 'The Amphibious Queen,' did some fancy work, and then Little Alice went through some very clever tumbling feats. Professor Beaumont was immersed for 3 mins. 28 sec.'

His act on other occasions might involve drinking a bottle of milk underwater, or he might escape from a weighed sack in which he had been tied or he might pick up over forty coins from the bottom of the tank, store them in his mouth and then surface to count them out in front of the astonished audience. I know how you feel. How you wish you could have been there.

Eventually Walter claimed to hold five world records. He said he held the record for saving lives from drowning, the world record for picking up coins from the bottom of a tank, '*the best record in the world for scientific and ornamental swimming*' and he said he was the fastest swimmer in the world, holding the 100 yards record. Oh yes, and he also claimed another world record by staying underwater for 4 minutes 35 seconds at the Alhambra Theatre in Melbourne in December 1893. Afterwards he was examined by a doctor who said that the circulation had stopped in his head above the ears, a condition which didn't seem to trouble him much. Walter said that he felt fine and went straight to his dressing room, after lifting a tired daughter out of the tank.

Exciting as this was, life didn't always go swimmingly. In 1888 he was summoned in a paternity case by one of his swimming troupe, Lily Mason. She was nineteen and was demanding maintenance for a child. He denied it was his, though he had previously sent his brother to try and buy her off. She told the court that his behaviour was a little unsettling. He could sometimes be found hiding under the beds of the girls in the swimming troupe, which generally is not conducive to a restful night's sleep. He explained his difficulties by telling the court that he was concerned that the diving tank was cracked and he was worried about how it could be replaced. The judge smiled sympathetically and ordered him to pay maintenance of five shillings a week.

Of course, as a performer you live and die by your publicity and his schemes sometimes got him into trouble. In 1890, ten year old Alice was detained on a charge of disorderly conduct, when she began to undress prior to jumping into the Thames from London Bridge in a publicity stunt. Her parents were charged with aiding and abetting by Detective Roper who had intervened, announcing rather grandly, '*I am a police officer and shall stop her going over this bridge.*' A crowd had gathered and the Beaumont's argued, quite convincingly, that any obstruction had actually been caused by the policeman arresting them. And anyway what was the problem? Alice was a professional swimmer who had been throwing herself off Llandudno Pier for years.

The judge was less charitable. He could not understand how they could endanger Alice's life *'simply for the sake of notoriety or pecuniary advantage.'* They were bound over to keep the peace for six months. But launching themselves off bridges was what the family did. Walter himself once dived from a height of 82 feet from the top of Conwy Bridge to raise money for the families of four boatmen who drowned in the estuary.

Walter Beaumont eventually gave up touring and settled in Llandudno in 1895 where, in addition to acting as the ever-alert lifeguard and offering swimming lessons, he and Alice gave afternoon exhibitions of *'ornamental swimming'* in the sea and high diving from the pier. He would treat the crowd to his *'Handcuff Dive,'* when he would dive into the sea secured in police handcuffs like Houdini, and then surface with his hands free. His *'Fire Dive'* was performed at twilight. He would be wrapped in a sack which was set alight and then thrown into the sea .He would then emerge like Neptune from the depths. He continued to amaze the public with his underwater displays in the glass-sided tank in the Egyptian Hall at the Pier Pavilion. where he sometimes challenged young men in the audience to submerge themselves in his tank and then peel an apple underwater in a race against the clock or, presumably, against drowning.

He was given the rather grand title of *'Rescuer of the Beach'* by the Town Commissioners of Llandudno in 1903, when he was presented with an illuminated scroll for saving of 113 people from drowning in his lifetime, including, in 1897, a sheep which chose to run into the sea rather than continue its march to the butchers. How grateful the sheep was for the Professor's intervention isn't recorded. He was also official keeper of the town dog, *'Jack Brown,'* though he was prosecuted for allowing it to wander around Llandudno unattended. He eventually became a member of the

Urban District Council but he could do little to improve his own finances.

There was little money to be made by holding your breath for long periods and, as Walter became older, he moved into hotel management. He took over the Kings Head pub in 1898 but he was not a businessman and bankruptcy proceedings for debts amounting to £596, were eventually brought against him in 1910 by the brewers Ind Coope. Bankruptcy cannot have come as a surprise, as it was revealed that '*he kept no books or accounts and had been aware of his insolvency for six or seven years.*' Walter blamed his problems on ill-health and was bemused by the laughter in court when he told them that he bet large sums on horses, but only when the horse told him it was going to win. He was as shocked as you are to discover that horses have the capacity to lie.

When he died in 1924, Walter was living quietly as the licensee of the Ferry Hotel in Tal-Y-Cafn in the Conwy Valley. He also operated a small pleasure craft on the River Conwy and they say that on the day it ran into difficulties, Walter made sure that everyone was returned safely to the river bank. However, he was in the cold water for much too long. He caught a chill and died. He was 69.

How can you sum up such an unusual life, the sort of life that it would be so unlikely today?' He found a vocation which suited him perfectly. Not everyone manages to do that, but Walter was never so happy or so comfortable as when he was in the water. Everybody, he said, should learn to swim, for swimming was just as easy as walking. If he had a journey to go he would rather swim it than walk.

Perhaps, though, I should leave the last word with the people of Llandudno. The newspaper said of him

'*A more useful life's work than that of Professor Beaumont it would be hard to find.*'

74

Llanelidan, Denbighshire
John Jones 1913

Coch Bach y Bala

Leave Ruthin on the A494 and travel south towards Corwen, then turn to the left and drive gently uphill to find a beautiful and unexpected valley. Here is Llanelidan, a place that seems untouched, overlooked, unchanged even, and because of that, more connected with the past than some other places. It probably wasn't much different when they laid him to rest.

Coch Bach y Bala, the little Redhead from Bala,

To find Coch Bach y Bala, you will need to visit the Church of St Elidan and look underneath two yew trees at the back of the cemetery. Just follow the main path from the lovely gate, walk around to the back and you will find his grave on the left hand side. It is low black slate and it carries his name. John Jones. Coch Bach y Bala. 1854 – 1913. A simple uncomplicated message, marking the end of a chaotic life.

Coch Bach y Bala, the little Redhead from Bala, John Jones. He was born in Merionethshire in about 1853 and he achieved a notoriety as a criminal and a folk hero. His exploits, eagerly reported by the press, captured the popular imagination. He was known as many things, including *The Little Welsh Terror* and *The Little Turpin*.

His reputation was fuelled by the press, who turned him into a countryside hero, a free spirit. People were happy to buy into this illusion. Yet what was he? Nothing much more than a petty criminal, an anti-social thief who did time in most of the prisons in North Wales and in England too. He tried a number of different jobs in his time – bricklayer, joiner, seaman, stoker - but he couldn't get on with any of them. They were too structured. He probably had to follow instructions. And regular employment didn't exploit his gifts. What he was good at was stealing, and he was devoted to refining his skills in this area of expertise.

From his earliest years, Jones continually stole anything he could take, things that were often of no use to him at all. He would store them in hedges and walls, to be collected later. The thieving magpie. Steal it first and then find out whether it would be useful later. In fact, he would often boast of stealing things that he hadn't, in an attempt to boost his reputation as north Wales' leading criminal. But a successful one wouldn't have spent quite as long behind bars as he did.

Until he was 17, he received brisk corporal punishment for his crimes, but in 1871 he went to grown-up prison for the first time for a month for poaching. A year later he was back inside for 4 months, this time for stealing a knife and an empty purse. In 1873, he stole 13 shillings and was imprisoned for 6 years. Poor John had found the place where he belonged and it was called prison.

The law always caught up with John Jones and eventually he would accumulate 10 separate convictions for theft, breaking and entering and for rioting against the police in Bala, when he threw stones at them. You see, he didn't like the police very much; they wouldn't leave him alone. Strangely, his subsequent behaviour in prison was generally very good, and he was usually released early on licence. He wasn't a problem. Apart, of course, from this tendency to escape. He first escaped from Ruthin Gaol in November 1879. He was awaiting trial for stealing fifteen watches in Bala. He opened his own cell and those of three others, before walking out through the main door. The staff were busy eating their supper at the time, so it wasn't their fault, obviously. Jones was on the run for three months. He was eventually re-arrested whilst he was in bed in the Swan Inn near Colwyn Bay, following a tip off. As a result, he was imprisoned for 14 years, probably in Dartmoor, a place that was to become his only home.

His second attempted escape followed his conviction at Beaumaris for stealing £10 from the Waterman's Arms in Amlwch. He was in Caernarfon Gaol, waiting to be transferred to Dartmoor again. John Jones was not a happy prisoner, since he was adamant hadn't done anything. And whilst he often boastfully claimed responsibility for crimes he hadn't committed, he now made such a fuss when the police themselves followed his example. He barricaded the door of his cell with parts of a weaving loom that was in there and started digging a tunnel.

He was not successful.

There were occasions when an unreasonable rage would come over him, which was probably a consequence of the mental instability that his behaviour so clearly illustrates. In 1906 he was convicted of burglary and of vicious assaulting a 71 year old woman. He kept the court sitting until 3.00 am, whilst he conducted his own defence and addressed the court. On this occasion he was sent to Dartmoor for 7 years. He was released in January 1913. This proved to be his last visit.

You see, the story has a tragic ending, as these stories often do. John Jones was 60 years old and had spent more than half of his life in prison, a life wasted in dark, damp and forbidding cells. And then, on 30 September 1913, he found himself in Ruthin Gaol once more. He had been convicted at Dolgellau Quarter Sessions and received a three year sentence, this time for breaking and entering Jordan's the Solicitors in Bala. The police had arrested him and put him in the lock-up in Dolgellau whilst awaiting trial but he escaped, and they found him in a barn three miles away. After his sentencing, he was given another opportunity to enjoy the secure surroundings of Ruthin Gaol, prior to beginning his sentence in Stafford Prison. Previous experience would suggest that Ruthin wasn't a place he liked very much. This time he tunnelled out of his cell and escaped over the roof of the chapel and the kitchen, using knotted sheets as a ladder, in traditional fashion. The North Wales Times was delighted.

John Jones effected his escape from Ruthin Prison on Tuesday morning, in a sensational manner. He gained his liberty as the result of indomitable pluck, great astuteness and wonderful ability. Coch Bach is regarded by some as a hero; his performance is certainly a daring piece of work. The daring manner of his escape and the quickness with which he left behind him the precincts of the prison baffled the gaol authorities and the police.

Coch Bach y Bala was always good copy, a journalist's dream. He spent the next week some miles away, living rough on the Nantyclwyd Estate. Here, he was pursued as if he were a piece of game, a target, a bit of sport. He was shot in the leg by one of the hunters, Reginald Jones-Bateman who was 19 years old. Coch Bach y Bala bled to death in the grass. Jones-Bateman was charged with manslaughter but he had money and the charge was dropped.

His funeral was quite an event, especially with local feeling running so high against the boy with the gun, for he was the son of an unpopular landlord. In shooting John Jones, he appeared to have been shooting one of his tenants, who came from the same stock and the same Welsh heritage as Coch Bach y Bala. After all, Jones–Bateman was not generally a surname shared by many on the hill farms of North Wales. Postcards were sold of the place where he was shot and of his funeral, attended by the sort of well-dressed people whose houses he had threatened. But finally, the Welsh Houdini had been trapped and confined in his grave.

Oh yes, John Jones, kleptomaniac and poacher, was a colourful character. A good story. A bit of a laugh. The sort of rebel who seems to fight back on behalf of the little man, against the system that suppressed them. A vagabond perhaps, but a loveable rogue. But he wasted the only life he had. And you wouldn't have wanted him moving into the house next door to you.

Llanelltyd, Dolgellau, Gwynedd
Frances Power Cobbe 1904

A valiant champion of the oppressed, both man and beasts.

Francis Power Cobbe was one of the most remarkable women of the nineteenth century and, when she died in April 1904, the terms of her will contained a very specific clause. She left instructions for a surgeon.

to perform on my body the operation of completely and thoroughly severing the arteries of the neck and windpipe (nearly severing the head altogether) as to render any revival in the grave absolutely impossible.

Like many Victorians, she had a profound dread of being buried alive and then regaining consciousness within a coffin, deep underground. Her fear, she said, had been provoked by the story of her great-grandmother, who apparently revived during her own funeral as a young girl and later married and gave birth to twenty-two children.

So the procedure was carried out as requested and, her death beyond dispute, she was laid to rest in a quiet grave in the cemetery of St Illtyd's church in Llanelltyd near Dollgellau, alongside her companion and partner, the sculptor Mary Lloyd.

She had left other instructions too.

I desire that my coffin be not made of oak, or of any durable wood but, on the principle of earth to earth burials, of the lightest and most perishable materials, merely sufficient to carry my body decently to the grave. I desire to be carried to Llanelltyd Cemetery, not in a funeral hearse, but in one or other of my own carriages, driven by my coachman, at his usual pace. And I desire that neither then, nor at any other time, may my friends or servants wear mourning for me.

Campaigner, journalist, social reformer and suffragette, she was a remarkable woman and, in so many things, a woman well ahead of her times. As her gravestone says, *'Bless her for her noble and unselfish life …a valiant champion of the oppressed, both man and beasts'.*

She was born in Ireland in December 1822 into a prominent family which apparently had previously produced five archbishops. Frances was the youngest of five children and was brought up within a devout Christian tradition, but she soon developed an alarming independence of thought. She found boarding school in Brighton uninspiring and largely educated herself, whilst looking after her ailing mother.

On the death of her parents, she used her legacy to travel independently around Europe and the Middle East. After contributing pieces about her travel experiences to magazines, she soon developed a career as a journalist in London, advocating social change, particularly with regards to women's rights. She campaigned with other leading feminists and wrote a pamphlet called *Wife Torture in England,* which exposed the domestic abuse some women experienced. She later wrote in her biography, *'I laboured to obtain protection for unhappy wives, beaten, mangled, mutilated or trampled on by brutal husbands.'* Her work was regarded as an important contributory factor in the Matrimonial Causes Act of 1878, which allowed abused women the right of legal separation on the grounds of assault.

Her own experiences as an intellectually frustrated young woman encouraged her to campaign for economic independence for women, in a celebrated piece called *Criminals, Idiots, Women and Minors,* in which she argued that without such independence, men would be able to sustain female suppression in the same way that they controlled *'criminals, idiots and minors'* and by so doing prevent emancipation.

Frances Cobbe was always driven by a desire to give a voice to the voiceless and began to channel her campaigning enthusiasm to the issue of animal rights – and it is for her work with the Anti-Vivisection League that she is perhaps best remembered. She had been troubled by animal experiments she had seen in Florence in 1863 and she saw an obvious connection between male brutality to animals and the subjection and abuse of women. Both women and animals, she argued, were similarly considered irrational and inferior. Just as children and women were dependent on husbands and fathers, so animals were completely reliant on humans. And all were therefore vulnerable as a result.

She was enraged by vivisection, the practice of dissecting animals, whilst they were still alive, for the purposes of scientific study. In 1870 she began to campaign against the mistreatment of animals and called for the introduction of laws to guarantee greater protection for any used in experiments. She condemned the church for its silence on such cruelty, seeing an evident contradiction in the concept of a loving God and acceptance of animal abuse. A piece she wrote called *Vivisection in America*, complete with horrific descriptions of abusive practices, became notorious.

In 1875, Cobbe founded the Society for the Protection of Animals Liable to Vivisection and its work resulted in Cruelty to Animals Act of 1876. As far as she was concerned however, it did not go far enough, since it did not end animal experimentation, but at least it introduced a level of control. She then founded the British Union for the Abolition of Vivisection in 1898. She was always highly regarded for her formidable intelligence and her commitment to sincerely held beliefs. Of course, she made herself very unpopular. Indeed in an act of revenge towards the end of her life she herself was accused by her opponents of cruelty to horses, which led to a lengthy court case – at the end of which the accusation was dismissed as an *absurd and ridiculous charge.*

She was regarded as eccentric, dressing *'in a masculine style'* and described by male writers as possessing *'great bodily size.'* She was always forthright and sometimes confrontational but the author

Louisa May Alcott said that when Frances was around, *'it was as if a great sunbeam had entered the room.'* When talking about herself she said, *'I have inherited a physical frame which, however defective even to the verge of grotesqueness from the aesthetic point of view, has been, as regards health and energy, a source of endless enjoyment to me.'* Whilst she regarded herself as overweight, she was happy to say, *'I could always entertain myself with my knife and fork!'*

She acknowledged that found no attraction in men and said that no man had ever been attracted by her. More importantly, however, Frances formed a marriage with sculptor Mary Lloyd, whom she met in Rome in 1861 and lived with from 1864 for over thirty years. She referred to Mary alternately as *'husband,' 'wife,'* and *'dear friend.'* The couple retired to Hengwrt, Mary's ancestral home near Dolgellau, in 1884. Frances continued to write prodigiously for newspapers and journals. In the six years between 1886 and 1892, she wrote 173 pamphlets for the Anti-Vivisection Society. She published her autobiography, *The Life of Frances Power Cobbe by Herself* (1894) which begins with *'My life has been an interesting one to live.'*

Mary Lloyd died in 1896 and was buried in Llanelltyd churchyard in the grave they would share. Rather poignantly I think, Frances wrote after her burial *'I have planted quantities of roses and other plants over it and over the high old wall behind, under which I have placed a seat.'* That seat is still there, weather-beaten but intact.

Frances herself died at Hengwrt on 5 April 1904. After her wishes were fulfilled, she was buried alongside Mary beneath a shared headstone. It is a beautiful place, with views to Cader Idris and down towards the sea.

Their gravestone has suffered over the years in that relentless North Wales weather but it has been revived by the addition of a brass plaque. Sadly Mary is not included and any hint of her name has long since eroded. However, a more fitting memorial to her can be found in the moving poem Frances wrote on Mary's death,

which ends

In joy and grief, in good and ill,
Friend of my heart: I need you still,
My Guide, Companion, Playmate, Love,
To dwell with here, to clasp above,
I want you,- Mary.

For O! if past the gates of Death
To me the Unseen openeth Immortal joys, to angels given,
Upon the holy heights of Heaven,
I'll want you,- Mary.

Frances Power Cobbe in St Illtyd's church, Llanelltyd

84

Llanfair, Caernarfon
Mary and Ellen Rogers 1843

With the intention of doing them good

We were scraping away the moss that covered the graves in St Mary's Churchyard in Llanfair-is-Gaer, on the banks of the Menai, with the endless flow of the tide alongside us, washing away the memories. We had been attracted by the sense of prosperity in this cemetery up against the sea. Sea captains, the customs man, the butcher from Hole in the Wall Street in Caernarfon, all lay here in the rough and uneven ground, amongst broken chest tombs and drifts of pretty snowdrops. And then, suddenly, the stone for which we had been looking, the resting place of Mary Jane Rogers, 18 months old and Ellen Emily Rogers, 9 weeks.

Their gravestone is in the centre of this photograph

Their gravestone has fallen and is partly obscured by grass, next to a large and overwhelming conifer. Two little girls, now alone and neglected, close to the church door. Their story, fading away to the sound of the wind, the waves and the gulls, is outlined on their tomb.

Beneath this stone are lowly laid
Two lovely babes as ever breathed.
They poisoned were and from their mother torn,
Both lived and died the very same morn.

No one comes to see them now.

They were a prosperous family, living on Bangor Street, within the city walls of Caernarfon and John and Ann Rogers employed a nurse to look after their two daughters. She was called Ellen Griffiths. When she eventually appeared in court she said

'I am guilty of administering laudanum to the children but I did so with the intention of doing them good.'

Poor Ellen. Once she had given it to them there was no going back. All she wanted was a bit of peace but once they had taken it, she could do nothing but watch them die.

All of us who are parents would have some understanding of her predicament. Children, seemingly beyond comfort, crying and crying. It is a sound from which there is no escape. It penetrates instinctively to your heart. There are times when, for a moment, you might do anything to stop it. And so two little girls were poisoned. There may have been no criminal intent, but they died all the same.

On the night of Saturday 30 September 1843, Mrs Rogers gave Ellen three half pennies to buy gin to make a punch for the girls. Mary Jane had been unwell and was getting a little cross. It was common practice to offer a little gin to bring a peaceful night's

86

sleep to both adult and child. After all, everyone feels better after a good night's sleep. There are those who still do such things today. But Mrs Rogers was adamant throughout. She never mentioned laudanum; it was gin she sent for.

Laudanum was a popular opium-based product in the nineteenth century, made by combining opium and alcohol. It was generally used for pain relief and to induce sleep. It was widely prescribed to both infants and adults. It had the advantage of being cheaper than gin, because it was regarded as medication, rather than as an alcoholic drink. Today in the UK, it is regarded as a Class A substance under the Misuse of Drugs Act but in the nineteenth century it was widely available and often given to children. Overdose and death were not unusual.

Ellen did not go out for the gin. She sent another servant, Jane Hughes, to buy a pennyworth of laudanum from Mr. Williams. More effective than gin, and cheaper too. A half penny saved. Mr. Williams remembered quite clearly selling a dram, but he didn't issue any instructions about its use. It had been market day and things were very busy. It was an adult dose he sold, but a deadly one for a child. The court heard that 8 to 15 minims or drops would kill a child. And in a dram there were 60 minims.

Ellen gave Mary Jane the laudanum in undiluted form and then rinsed out the cup she used, to give baby Ellen Emily her share.

Did she know what she was doing? Or was she caught out by her own ignorance?

Ann saw Mary Jane at 8.00 pm. She appeared to have settled. However, by the early hours Ann became concerned enough to send for Doctor William Roberts. But poor Mary Jane died at 6.30 am before he arrived.

Ellen Emily had been a healthy child but that night became very drowsy. She had convulsions and turned *'a livid hue.'* They managed to calm her slightly by bathing her in warm water but by 7.00 am she, too, was dead.

The inquest was held on Monday in the house of Captain Griffiths. The jury went off to Bangor Street to inspect the bodies, along with the reporter from *The Caernarfon and Denbigh Herald*.

They lay as in sleep, save that the features of the elder child bore manifest tokens of the convulsive death throes, whilst those of the younger were so calmly, so softly sweet, so severely tranquil, as almost to induce the hope that she yet slumbered. Death however had too surely done his work, and scarce an eye could refrain from the tribute of tears.

At first Ellen could not face the enormity of what she had done. She denied everything, then admitted giving the baby the drug but said that Mary Jane had had only gin. Dr Roberts claimed that had he known what had happened in the first place, he might have been able to save the baby, but the delays had been critical.

The Coroner was forthright in his view. Ellen Griffith's actions had been reckless in the extreme. She had acted with neither knowledge nor authority. She had to stand trial. When this was translated from English into Welsh for her, she fell into hysterics. *'Her fits were very severe and lasted for many hours'*. She *'exhibited the most intense agony.'* Eventually in the evening she was taken to Mr. George, the governor of the County Gaol, where she remained until her trial in March 1844.

When those Assizes began the Judge, Sir John Williams, immediately summarised the legal position. The charge could not be murder, for he was sure there was *'no malice or design to take away life or to do any injury.'* However the law must act. She was tried for manslaughter and although she admitted what she had done, she pleaded not guilty. It was a vain attempt to escape punishment. There was never any argument about what had happened and, inevitably, she was found guilty.

Williams told her that she had ignored her duty to provide due care and caution. No servant was *'permitted ignorantly to trifle with the lives of those children who might be committed to their care.'* However, her previous good character was acknowledged and, since she had been imprisoned since September 1843, she would only be detained further until the end of the Assizes.

There was no criminal negligence, just deadly ignorance in using a remedy employed by others but which she did not understand. Perhaps she was not alone in this. The editorial in the *Caernarfon and Denbigh Herald* spoke strongly against the practice of using either gin or laudanum. It spoke eloquently, but too late, of accidents waiting to happen.

Ellen Griffiths, as far as I can tell, now slips from history, but I am sure those inescapable visions of convulsive children dying in front of her with purple faces never left her.

The gravestone. St Mary's Church. Llanfair

They now rest where Agricola, the Roman general, crossed over to Anglesey by fording the Menai Strait. Look for the old St.

89

Mary's Church in Llanfair. Leave the A487 between Bangor and Caernarfon at a roundabout signposted the *Plas Menai National Water Sports Centre* and you will find the church in front of you on the very edge of the sea. Their stone lies on the grass to the left of the church door, beneath a large conifer.

Their gravestone is in local slate and is still clearly legible. *'Sacred to the memory of Mary Jane Aged 1 Year and 7 months and Ellin (sic) Emily, aged 9 weeks.'* The sad little verse lies at the bottom, an inadequate symbol of a family confronting unimaginable grief.

Please visit the girls if you can. Who knows what they might have become if Mary hadn't been cross?

Llanfoist, Gwent
Crawshaw Bailey 1872

Did you ever see such a funny thing before?

Cosher Bailey had an engine.

He had lots of other things too. His real name was Crawshaw Bailey and ran ironworks at Rhymney; he constructed tramways; he operated a railway company; he owned brickworks. He bought up large expanses of coal fields at their agricultural value in the Rhondda and at Mountain Ash and then exploited the huge resources beneath to make enormous profits when the price was right. He was High Sheriff of Brecknock, then later of Monmouthshire; he was an MP for 16 years.

He was born in Suffolk in 1789. His uncle was Richard Crawshay, the iron master of Cyfartha Castle in Merthyr, and Crawshaw Bailey was sent to work there when he was 12. Of course, there were very many other twelve year olds in the works at this time, but their expectations and their treatment were entirely different. Crawshaw was part of a dynasty. He went into the iron business with his brother Joseph in 1811 at Nantyglo when he was 22 and became seriously rich.

That wealth did not spread far. The men who created his wealth lived in shocking conditions in the middle of a devastated moonscape. It was called the Blackened Valley. Sulphurous smoke made the daytime sky yellow and the nights glowed red, like an image of hell. This was a world pillaged. Eleven seams of coal were worked. 150 miles of tramway were laid. And, in the middle of it all, people lived. Workers houses were built and owned by the company and were generally without any kind of sanitation. But there was nowhere else to live, or indeed to work. If a worker was made redundant, then he lost his home.

The *truck* or company shop established even greater control over workers and provided additional income for the ironmasters. Workers were paid with tokens that could only be redeemed in company shops, where prices were considerably higher than elsewhere. Sometimes, if there was a cash-flow issue, then workers were paid in goods from the shop. Debt was inevitable. Lodgers had to be taken in to support income and children were sent out to work at the age of seven. As early as 1830, the Monmouthshire magistrates petitioned the House of Commons, requesting the abolition of company shops because they were serious threat to the maintenance of peace.

From our modern perspective, it seems that workers lived in conditions of slavery. Industrial relations were based upon ruthlessness. Wages rose and fell in line with fluctuations in the price of iron, a shocking idea for those who lived on the edge of destitution. Trade unions were illegal, although Friendly Societies were allowed, since they were largely benevolent, providing sickness or death benefit. However, in these circumstances, it is not a surprise that the workforce became increasingly radical and very soon Nantyglo developed a reputation for rebellion.

The first attempt to organise workers was made by the *Scotch Cattle* who appeared in 1822. Their objective was to prevent '*strangers*' taking jobs in mining. They blackened their faces and wore animal skins and would visit the homes of those working during strikes or co-operating with mine owners to punish them, by ransacking their property and making threats. It was the potato famine that prompted this, for it drove many out of Ireland, who were ready to work at even lower wages than those normally offered. Ironmasters were happy to employ them too, thus setting workers against each other. These were desperate times.

Chartism emerged in the late 1830s and one of the leading figures was Zephenia Williams, the landlord at the *Royal Oak Inn* in Nantyglo. Crawshaw Bailey wanted all Chartists to be thrown into the works pond and agreed with the other ironmasters to refuse employment to known Chartists. *The Royal Oak* was declared out of bounds to all Bailey's employees. For their part, Chartists gathered muskets and pikes, forged secretly in the works, and hid them in remote caves in the hills.

It was in such a fearful atmosphere that the Nantyglo Round Towers were built. They are still, quite simply, remarkable.

On Roundhouse Farm

You will find them at Roundhouse Farm, constructed by the Bailey brothers about a mile away from the iron works. They had originally built a mansion called Ty Mawr, close to the source of their wealth. The house faced away from the works and they obscured the view at the back as much as they could with trees. Ty Mawr was finished in 1816. In that year there was considerable industrial unrest – there was a riot when the Baileys threatened to reduce workers' wages. That threat was withdrawn, but then implemented six years later. On this occasion workers attempted to stop coal from entering the furnaces. A group of workers attacked local militiamen and a detachment of soldiers were billeted in the barn at Roundhouse Farm.

The Towers were constructed and fortified as a refuge for the Baileys in the event of revolution. Their very own panic room; a place to stay safe until the soldiers came to rescue them. In a way, that makes them part of the last castle to be built in Britain. It was believed that there was an underground passage linking Ty Mawr and the towers, though this has never been found. There were barns and stables for the horses that were used in the works to haul trucks along tramways. In fact a tram way ran through the farmyard. Soon the farm was enclosed within a substantial wall. Entrance was through enormous iron gates.

'I owe all that I have to my own industry.' said Crawshaw Bailey rather ingenuously, *'and I would risk my life rather than lose my property.'* He was ready for anything. There were substantial ventilated cellars for the storage of provisions in the case of a prolonged siege. There are gun loops in the iron door.

The south west tower is now largely a ruin but the other is more intact. The most astonishing thing about the construction is that there hardly any wood used anywhere. Apart from the stone, everything is made of iron. For an ironmaster it had two benefits. Firstly, iron was much cheaper than wood. Secondly, it was the perfect expression of a huge ego. The internal support beams and the 'A' frame roof are iron. The window frames, the sills, the lintels, everything. There are even cast iron horse troughs. And the iron was treated as if it was wood. Joists are joined to beams using dove-tail joints.

The roof is made up of 20 cast iron segments which were overlaid with pitch and bricks, which have now started to give way. The walls of stone were four feet thick, topped with small crenelations. It is the only known farm building in the world that was built in this way.

An iron window frame in the tower

The place is a unique part of our heritage, a reminder of the bitter hostility that existed between the ironmasters and their workers. These were cruel and exploitative times and to many, these towers are a monument to tyranny. They stood as a symbol of power to intimidate, just as the castles of Edward 1 had done in Wales centuries before.

Bailey retired from the works in about 1850 and moved to Llanfoist House where he died in 1872. He never saw The Nantyglo ironworks being dismantled in 1878.

The history of Nantyglo defined by the growth and the decline of the iron and coal industries, and Crawshaw Bailey is at the heart of it. Of course, he is remembered in an interminable song, *Cosher Bailey's Engine*, with that irritatingly memorable chorus, these days only ever sung on coach trips -

Did you ever see such a funny thing before.

In St Faith's Churchyard, Llanfoist

Bailey is buried down in Llanfoist, in the comfort of the Usk Valley. His grave is marked by a brown marble obelisk in the cemetery next to the A478 outside Abergavenny. Up there in Nantyglo life was much harder. And no, I have never seen anything like Roundhouse Farm before.

> *Yes, Cosher Bailey he did die*
> *And they put him in a coffin*
> *But, alas, they heard a knocking*
> *Cosher Bailey, only joking*

Notice the use of the word *alas*. You can understand why people were anxious that he was in his coffin – and that he was going to stay there. But perhaps his descendants live on secretly. There were always stories in Nantyglo, stories about desperate men being given jobs in the works and their grateful wives suddenly having red-headed babies nine months later. Bailey had red hair you see…

Llangrannog, Ceredigion
Sarah Jane Rees
1916

The Navigator Lady

St Carannog's Church, with Sarah's tomb at the back

Her grave stands in a prominent position at the very back of St. Cranog's churchyard in Llangrannog, right in the centre of the village. It lies between Aberystwyth and Cardigan, and you reach this village that faces the sea, down a steep hill from the busy A487. Sarah's is an imposing tomb, topped by a black urn, a symbol in Victorian graveyards of generosity, which is so appropriate for a woman who gave so much to others. Now she looks down towards the narrow little streets like a benevolent teacher, which is, of course, what she was.

The inscription is, quite rightly in Welsh. It reads

*She stood on her own amongst the women
and wives of the nation in genius and talent.
Her character was without blemish and she lectured,
preached and wrote for over 50 years.*

The tight and narrow community of Llangrannog tumbles down steeply to a pebble beach and rough seas. It is an isolated place, intense perhaps, and when you look at the sea crashing on to the rocks, it is hard to imagine that anyone could actually launch a boat from this little cove, let alone navigate around the dangerous coastline. Yet Sarah could. It was here that she began her journeys.

She was a great achiever and those who rush down to the sea in this pretty village don't give her a second glance. Yet she was a remarkable woman. Master mariner, teacher, a crowned bard, preacher, lecturer. Given her humble origins, her achievements are astonishing.

She died in 1916 at the age of seventy-seven, after a lifetime defined by a mission to educate and improve the lives of those around her. If you find her photograph, you can see a proud woman, confident and comfortable, but with an undeniable spark in her eyes, ready to confront and defy expectations. She was a prominent member of her own community and of the wider world of West Wales. No one could accuse her of wasting her life.

She was born in 1839 into a confined life on a small farm but at least her horizons were not as narrow as those of many of her contemporaries. Her boundaries encompassed the sea. Her father navigated a small boat up and down the coast as a self-employed trader. He was a successful one and the family soon moved up in the world. They wanted Sarah to become a dressmaker but her ambitions were far more exciting. She wanted an education. She became a Band of Hope leader and a Sunday School teacher. She went to colleges for Ladies in Liverpool and in Chester and then finally to a nautical school in London. And, as a result, she qualified as a sea captain and was awarded a master's certificate. Indeed, she was the first British woman to get a Board of Trade ticket. She was a highly skilled navigator and the theory she acquired filled in the background to all those practical experiences she had with her father on his boat as a child. As a result she became a prominent figure when she returned to live in her own community. She commanded considerable respect in this old fashioned, male dominated world.

Sarah became a teacher at Pontgarreg School and later head teacher. She was a particularly talented teacher of music who supported vigorously the Tonic Sol fa system of notation that helped reluctant Sunday School singers for generations. All her life was devoted to others, especially women and the under privileged. So she took education out into the community, teaching in barns and other farm buildings and village halls.

The arrival of train lines in West Wales opened up this isolated part of the country to the rest of the world and it was important that the horizons of the people expanded in a similar way through education. The old ways, that restricted women and denied opportunities to children, needed to change. Sarah saw that expanding education was the way in which to do this. So she taught basic literacy and numeracy skills to farm boys and advanced navigation to sea captains who came to the school after the children had gone home. She had both the theory and the background of sailing along this dangerous and rocky coast. It was a risky, fragile occupation, always watching the weather, the wind, the tide. And yet who was the best navigator? Who was the best teacher? Who knew the channels and the currents better than anyone else? Sarah Rees.

She used the respect she had gained in this hard-drinking world of mariners by promoting temperance. Sarah became very exercised by the role that alcohol played in these remote and isolated communities, as others did too. Many Welsh women campaigned against alcohol, blaming it for all moral and social ills. It was seen as a drain on the limited finances of the poor, punishing children and women, for money for food was allegedly spent in pubs. There were always grim days out in the west when the weather closed in and there was only the drink. In these tiny little communities, linked only by the sea, domestic violence was not unusual.

The North Wales Temperance Union was set up in Blaenau Ffestiniog and it spread quickly. Protests in pubs and on the street were organised. She started the Women's Temperance Union in South Wales in 1901, travelling as far as Tregaron in her pony and trap to promote her message. Temperance became very much a feminist issue and she was confident and firm of purpose. Her seamanship had already shown her that she could confront male expectations. She had never accepted the isolated and claustrophobic world of a remote Welsh village, nor had she ever embraced a forgotten life of drudgery. She believed quite firmly that women deserved better. It wasn't that she was concerned to ban alcohol all together, but the excessive consumption was intimately wedded to domestic violence, the abuse of women and the neglect of children.

The success and the excitement of their campaigns gave women the confidence to face other issues, like votes for women. The impact that women like Sarah Rees had therefore, was profound and long-lasting. Through the Temperance Union, women found a voice that would not be silenced. Her campaign for women's rights led her to establish a magazine to promote women writers. 'Y Frythones' (The Female Briton) was a significant publication, enabling women to participate in public events through the articles that they submitted. The first Welsh magazine for women was '*Y Gymraes*' (*The Welsh Woman*) which concentrated largely upon housekeeping issues. Sarah's magazine, appearing a few years later, promoted women's achievements and aspirations, rather than domestic hints and tips. The magazine began in 1879 and Sarah was editor for 12 years. As you can see in other parts of her life, education, both secular and religious, was of the utmost importance to her. This was reflected in the nature of the magazine. The role of women and their unfulfilled potential was something that she felt passionately about and through the magazine, women began to find a distinctive voice.

She succeeded in her own writing too. In 1865 she was the first woman to be awarded the chair of the Royal National Eisteddfod in Aberystwyth for her poem, '*Y Fodrwy Briodasol.*' In 1873 she won the chair in Aberaeron. She adopted the Eisteddfod tradition of a bardic name, one which paid homage to the village that made her – Cranogwen.

Sarah Jane Rees - Cranogwen

As she grew older, she gained the confidence to travel more widely. She lectured and preached in America, for example and the money she earned was donated to her village community – chapels were built, bridges repaired. Sarah was a woman with purpose and generosity who never forgot where she came from and was determined to throughout her life to put something back.

Following her death in 1916 a refuge for homeless women and girls in the Rhondda was established in her memory in 1922, Llety Cranogwen. And Aberystwyth University still has an open scholarship available in her memory, the Cranogwen award.

Sarah lives on. She was a remarkable and influential woman. And when you look at the black urn on her fine tomb at the back of the churchyard, you can only wish that your own life could be half as successful and influential as the life of Sarah Jane Rees of Llangrannog.

Llangynwyd, Mid Glamorgan
Wil Hopcyn 1741

The Maid of Cefn Ydfa

This is the grave of Wil Hopcyn which represents the story of Ann Maddocks, the Maid of Cefn Ydfa, and her doomed love for her bard. Their story is remembered in a folk song we all can recognise, *'Bugeilio'r Gwenith Gwyn,'* which established their reputation, amongst some anyway, as a kind of Welsh Romeo and Juliet.

Wil Hopcyn. The Welsh Romeo?

Cefn Ydfa was an impressive residence in the Llynfi Valley, about six miles north of Bridgend, where in the earliest years of the eighteenth century, William and Catherine Thomas had two children, a son who died in infancy and a daughter called Ann. When William died unexpectedly in 1706, three year old Ann suddenly, and unknown to herself, became a desirable heiress.

Wil Hopcyn came from a different class. He was born in Llangynwyd in 1700 and was a tradesman – a thatcher, a tiler, a plasterer - who met Ann when they were both in their twenties, during some maintenance work he carried out at Cefn Ydfa.

They say Ann would send the servants away from the kitchen at dinner time, so that she could talk to him. After all, he had a reputation as a silver-tongued devil, someone witty, articulate and romantic. This *'ripened into deep and passionate love.'* Inevitably such emotions could not be concealed forever and, also inevitably, they outraged Ann's mother. A rich heiress and a plasterer? How could that make sense? You might, indeed, have some sympathy for her views, depending of course, on the tradesman who have been to your own house. Certainly, the relationship was forbidden but they grasped at secret moments and would meet in the woods around the house, *'where the young people poured out their unavailing love.'* But these meetings couldn't remain secret and Ann was soon confined to her room, whilst her mother promoted a marriage to the favoured suitor, Anthony Maddocks, a solicitor. His ardour should perhaps be seen in another context. His father was a trustee with some responsibility over Ann and some believe that he made use of this position to engineer a marriage which would enable the Maddocks family to absorb the Cefn Ydfa estate. But then, it would be quite easy to question Wil's motives too, for marriage to an up-town girl and wealthy heiress would not have harmed the finances of a local labourer.

Love, though, will sometimes find a way and, with the help of a servant, Ann still corresponded with Wil - using the hollow of a large tree as a post box, like secret agents, where letters could be lodged. Once again their clandestine communications were uncovered. Her writing materials were confiscated and the story has it that Ann then wrote to Wil on a sycamore leaf, using a pin dipped in her own blood. She then *'trusted the precious love-token to the mercy and charge of the wind that wailed around her room, in the hope that the record of her love and suffering and constancy should reach his eyes.'* They never arrived, for the Welsh weather was as unreliable then as it is now. Mind you, if you prefer a more prosaic explanation, try the one that says her maid didn't take the messages but burnt them. It doesn't matter really, because the essential element in the story is that Wil, hearing nothing from her, believed he had been rejected, his love sacrificed on the altar of property. Ann heard nothing from him, either. Perhaps it was time to move on. Of such misunderstandings is a tragedy born.

So she married Anthony Maddocks on 5 May, 1725 and two years later Ann gave birth to a daughter who died - just a few days before she did.

Wil had gone to work in the docks at Bristol after he heard of her marriage and, in June 1727, he dreamt that Maddocks was dead. The dream, though, was a bitter deception. He rushed back to Cefn Ydfa to find that Maddocks was still alive and thriving, but that Ann was wrestling with fatal illness. When she cried out for her one true love, Anthony abandoned her. Her mother brought Wil to her and Ann fell into his arms. She died in his embrace. Her remains were interred in the chancel of Llangynwyd church, along with her father and brother. Anthony went on to marry a new heiress, who had the considerable advantage of being alive, and he now lies buried in the family tomb, outside the beautiful church of St Cynwyd.

Wil Hopcyn lived for a further fourteen years, but he never married. He died when he fell from a ladder, whilst working in Llangynwyd on 19 August 1741, and was buried close to the western yew tree in the churchyard. The stone which marked his grave was later used as a foundation for a neighbouring tomb.

He had however, expressed his heartbreak in a poem, sung to a haunting Welsh folk-tune, *'Bugeilio'r Gwenith Gwyn,'* which roughly translates as *'Watching the White Wheat.'* In it, Wil declared his undying love for someone who had abandoned him for another. Her beauty, which he had watched ripening like a field of corn, would be harvested by his rival.

> *I fondly watch the blooming wheat,*
> *And others reap the treasure.*

And that is where it sat for quite a while, just an old romantic story that had drifted some way away from what probably happened. There was a revival of interest in the story in 1846 but it really took off in 1869, when it was published in a popular collection of poems called *'The Cupid'* by Thomas Morgan from Maesteg, which were often recited on stage. It was followed in 1871 by a long letter to the Cambrian newspaper from Mrs. Penderel Llewellyn, *'the worthy vicar's wife'* in Llangynwyd, who was in the habit of putting flowers on Ann's grave. Some have blamed her for the whole thing, claiming that she invented it all – the real Wil Hopcyn was nothing more than a drunken beggar. For others, the point was that these were all real people, with gravestones. As such, the story became fixed in the national consciousness, *'the prettiest and most pathetic love-story in the whole history of Wales'* one journalist called it– and as such, people wanted to believe it. And why shouldn't they?

The story of the Maid of Ydfa came to represent the village of Llangynwyd, but towards the end of the nineteenth century the churchyard was described as *'one of the worst kept in the country.'* The remnants of Wil's headstone had been rescued by the composer Joseph Parry and placed near Ann but when the church was renovated by Olive Talbot of Margam Park, the gravestones were found in the chancel, covered by building materials.

In October 1892 a committee met at the Maesteg Post Office to raise funds to erect a monument to Ann, *'in keeping with the beautified interior of the church.'* They invited subscriptions and hoped to receive *'sufficient to erect a memorial over the grave of Wil Hopcyn, her humble but talented lover, who was buried under the yew tree on the western side of the old churchyard.'* They commissioned a dark marble slab, with brass plate inlaid, with Ann's name in a *'facsimile of the maid's handwriting.'* On one side of the plate you can see an engraving of wheat in bloom with a sickle and on the other side some sycamore leaves. The committee were so pleased with the design that, before it was installed, the brass was exhibited in the shop window of Mr. Williams, ironmonger in Bridgend. These are the memorials that we can see today - Ann in the chancel, and Wil in the churchyard under the shade of a yew tree. The original gravestones are in the bell tower of the church.

It is the old village of Llangynwyd you need to visit. They call it 'Top Llan' and it is up the hill from the A4063 that goes through the new village and into Maesteg. St Cynwyd has a tightly packed and surprisingly extensive cemetery, regarded as possibly the largest private graveyard in Europe. Wil though, is easy to find. He is still under that lovely old yew just outside the church door.

Wil and Ann are also remembered on the Hopcyn Cross, erected in 1927 to mark the bicentenary of Ann's death. It is outside the Corner House Inn, allegedly the site of Wil's home. Naturally he is now said to haunt the premises. Together they have inspired novels, an opera by Joseph Parry, an early silent film made in Wales in 1904 and rediscovered in a stairwell of a house near Swansea in 1984 and, of course, 'Bugeilio'r Gwenith Gwyn.' I could hum it for you but it might not go terribly well in a book. So listen to Catrin Finch playing it on the harp or find Mary Hopkin singing it on YouTube. That would be better.

Llysworney, South Glamorgan
The Murder of David Thomas 1885

He described it as the cleverest thing he had yet done

I had to move away the tired tentacle of a creeping bramble littering the tomb just to make sure. But there was no doubt. This was, indeed, the burial place of David Thomas and this grave, in St Tydfil's Church, represents a terrible crime which reached a truly horrible conclusion, quite at odds with the prosperous serenity of Llysworney.

The grave of David Thomas, Llysworney

It is a lovely tranquil village in the Vale of Glamorgan near Llantwit. A place for contemplation and reflection perhaps, whilst relaxing next to the duck pond and speculating on how you can help to make the world a better place. But that was not why David Thomas was buried here. He hadn't lived a long and fulfilled life in such a place that many of us would envy. Because David Thomas was only forty when he was murdered by David Roberts in 1885, in what became known as *'The Cowbridge Murder.'*

In October 1885, the farmer and cattle dealer David Thomas, went to Treorchy market. He lived at Stallcourt Farm at Llanblethian with his wife and four children and was well known in the area. He had spent some time in America and, inevitably perhaps, was known as *'The Yankee.'* He was regarded as a shrewd businessman who seemed always to have plenty of cash. In Treorchy he received £60 owed to him by a man called Jenkins, which included a distinctive sovereign with a hole in it. He had stuffed the money into a canvas bag, which he always carried with him, and then went off for a few convivial drinks with his chums before returning on the train to Cowbridge. Here he collected another debt from a local farmer and went off to celebrate a successful day at the *Duke of Wellington Inn* in the centre of town. Perhaps unwisely, he bought drinks freely, displaying not only his largesse but also his canvas bag full of cash. He waved it around and offered to lend anyone £20. This was not sensible.

This display of generosity in *The Duke of Wellington* was watched very closely by Edward Roberts, a sawyer, who lived near Stallcourt Farm in a small cottage with his son, David. Edward was not especially popular but David, who was 28, was feared as unpredictable and aggressive. Whilst he may have been devoted to his father, he was someone to be avoided. He had just returned from military service with the Royal Scots, though in reality he had spent most of his time in a military prison. He was insubordinate and had assaulted senior officers. Eventually, he had been discharged as *'incorrigible.'* The two of them tried to play cards with David Thpmas and his nephew John, but Edward was so drunk that he couldn't stay awake. At closing time they all staggered off together. Edward Roberts fell over twice and had to be picked up by his son. It was not a night in which to fall over either, for the weather was foul. High winds and heavy rain left paths underwater and turned fields into swamps.

And on a night such as this David Thomas never got home.

His body was found the next morning by a man going to work, 200 yards from Stallcourt Farm. He had shocking head wounds. He had been battered almost beyond recognition with a blunt object. There were also two lacerations to the front of his face. The police were called and the body was carried to his house on a ladder. David Roberts was one of the bearers.

David Thomas's nephew, John, was initially suspected of the crime but the police investigation quickly identified the Roberts family as the prime suspects and the two of them were arrested. They both denied any involvement and claimed not to have seen him at all that night. This was very quickly dismissed. They had been seen together by everyone else who had been in the *Wellington*. So their cottage was searched. A blood-stained handkerchief was found holding £66, including a sovereign with a hole in it. A blood-stained billhook was also found.

At the police station the Roberts's were over-heard trying to concoct an alibi. The money was their Christmas savings. '*I will tell them I was saving it up to buy a new suit of clothes or something of that sort.*'

David Roberts was undoubtedly a difficult and volatile person but he displayed complete devotion to his father and made a confession to the police. This was obviously an attempt both to exonerate his father completely, and to protect himself. He said he had taken his father home and put him to bed and then gone back out to intercept David Thomas. He had demanded money, they had struggled, he had hit him with a stick three times and Thomas had banged his head when he fell. He was clearly trying to minimise his actions, but the confession wasn't convincing. He didn't have the time to go home and deal with a drunken father before going back out to confront the victim who was so close to home. And he didn't use a stick. He slashed him with a billhook and battered his head with a rock. A stone covered in blood was found close to the body. It seemed probable that the old man was not willing to part with his money and that Roberts killed him in a frenzied attack. He may have confessed, but to the press it was clear that *'nothing can prevent the exaction of the inexorable demand of British Law.'*

Edward might well have been so drunk that he knew nothing of the attack but he was certainly there. So, despite the confession, they were both sent for trial. It was held in February 1886 and began with the acquittal of the father on the grounds of insufficient evidence of direct involvement in the murder and then moved quickly on to the death sentence for the son, based upon his confession. It was all over very quickly.

Awaiting his execution he wrote to his cousin *'I acknowledge my transgressions and my sins are ever before me.'* He also wrote to David Thomas's wife, asking for forgiveness. In the few weeks left to him he found religion and studied the Bible.

Berry, the executioner, travelled to Cardiff on St David's Day after hanging Thomas Nash, who had killed his daughter in Swansea. Berry was still relatively inexperienced.

Because David Roberts was a big man, they decided to make the drop quite a short one – which was a terrible error of judgement. As a consequence, it did not go well, as the press reported.

As morning on 2 March 1886 broke, *'small groups of the unwashed section of the public commenced to assemble in front of the gaol.'* The sky had a *'dull leaden look.'* Inside Roberts had passed a largely peaceful night and was led to the gallows before 8.00 am when *'the minute bell was solemnly tolling out the death knell'.* The execution was observed by four journalists, an obligation none of them relished.

Quickly the deed was done, but within a few seconds Roberts' chest began to heave and his limbs twitched violently. These convulsions continued for some time and, when the reporter for the Press Association produced his watch to time the agony, the journalists were escorted from the chamber. They did not witness the death of David Roberts.

The reporters later criticised the conduct of the execution at the inquest. Berry became angry, threatening to start immediate legal action for slander *'against anyone who circulated such a report.'* They could not know what had happened after they left, though the implication was that Berry pulled on the legs of the hanging man to finally break his neck. At the inquest officials were desperate to show that the neck was broken, and that death had been instantaneous. The movements seen were merely *'muscular contractions.'* The press, however, were convinced that they had witnessed a slow and painful death from strangulation.

'Having partaken of breakfast, Berry, who had meanwhile been talking wholly about the execution, which he described as the cleverest thing he had yet done, rose, shook hands with everybody and left to catch the Great Western 10.10 am train for the north.'

Mold, Flintshire
Richard Wilson 1782

Loggerheads

Richard Wilson in St Mary's Church, Mold

In Mold, by the north side of St. Mary's Church at the top of the town, you will find the chest tomb which contains the remains of the important Welsh landscape artist, Richard Wilson. He was a great and an influential painter, the *'father of English landscape painting,'* admired by Turner and Constable. Yet despite his talents and his considerable legacy, he died rejected and in poverty in North Wales.

He was the son of a Welsh clergyman, born on 1 August 1713

114

at Penegoes near Machynlleth . His family was well connected and his maternal uncle, Sir George Wynne, arranged for him to become a pupil of a leading painter, Thomas Wright, in 1730. He stayed there for six years, learning techniques and composition and developing his contacts. Wynne later helped him financially when he set up his own studio.

Wilson became a well-regarded portrait painter. He completed a portrait of Flora Macdonald on her release from the Tower of London, where she was imprisoned after helping Bonnie Prince Charlie to escape. He was invited to paint the Prince of Wales in 1748. He seemed destined to make a good living from his portraits and career path appeared clearly planned out for him. Wilson had a reputation as a fashionable man and opened his own studio in Covent Garden with the help of his new patrons, the Lyttleton family. They provided him with the financial support to go to Italy in 1750. It may have been a developing interest in landscape painting which drew him there, but it was certainly an experience which changed his life.

He first went to Venice and remained there for several months, where he studied the works of some of the great Italian artists in Venice and continued his work as a portrait painter. Wilson's interest in landscape was encouraged by the Venetian landscape painter, Francesco Zuccarelli, and the rich Englishman, William Lock became his patron. In 1751, Wilson left Venice with Lock and travelled to Rome. Here he continued to work for aristocratic English tourists, providing souvenirs of their grand European tour from his studio in the Piazza di Spagna. He painted some large landscapes in the style of Poussin and he also did numerous drawings of Roman sites and buildings which he used in composing Italianate landscapes after his return to England. He remained in Rome for six years.

On his return to England, Wilson opened an even grander studio than the one he had left. He became actively involved in founding first the Society of Artists and then the Royal Academy of Art, holding many exhibitions. But he was not always a popular figure and soon struggled to sell his work. A contemporary said '*inanimate nature proved but a cold patroness.*' Landscapes were regarded as very much second rate; it was in portrait painting where there was money to be made. Landscapes, which of necessity required the artist to tour around the country, were much more expensive to produce.

Gainsborough painted landscapes as a hobby, since he could make plenty of money from his portraits. But Wilson could not. They said that his work '*was not suited to English tastes.*' They said that his character was against him – that he had '*not courtesy or consideration and made enemies where he should have made friends.*' For example, when King George III suggested that 100 guineas might be a little expensive for a landscape, he suggested, unwisely I think, that the King could pay in weekly instalments if he couldn't afford it.

Wilson slipped quickly into poverty, leading a desperate life in squalid rooms on Tottenham Court Road, selling his work cheaply to pawnbrokers and art dealers. Wilson worked in his small bare room with an easel and only a single brush, re-designing and re-using existing canvases. He would produce replicas of his previous work to generate some income. He painted Niagara and the Acropolis without ever visiting them. Success, though, eluded him. On one occasion he had insufficient money to obtain the materials he needed to fulfil a commission. This desperation was all rather at odds with the sense of classical serenity his work often displayed.

In 1776 there was some respite when he was appointed as librarian at the Royal Academy, with a salary of £50 per year. This is generally believed to have saved him from starvation. In 1781 he returned to live with his cousin on a small estate at Colomendy outside Mold and it seemed that he had lived his life with his gifts neglected. He died a year later on 11 May 1782, aged 69.

His death led to a reassessment of his abilities. Soon he was regarded as the founder of English landscape painting. He was admired by both Turner and Constable for his '*grandeur of expression*' and the '*dignity of his mind.*' Constable said of him '*Poor Wilson! Think of his fate, think of his magnificence*' Wilson had seen some things differently. For him, the sky is no longer merely the background. In his work, it has life and creates atmosphere in the way that it would for later artists. You will notice, too, that they are the sort of dramatic skies which are common in North Wales.

He painted Welsh and English scenes, though sometimes they could really be anywhere. He gave his English and Welsh views a grand classical appearance as a result of his Italian experience. Some critics say that his pictures are very similar – a view seen through a frame of trees, with small figures in the foreground, dominated by the huge countryside, with an overall sense of tranquility.

There is a fine collection of his work in the National Museum of Wales. His greatest works are perhaps *The Summit of Cader Idris* which is in the Tate and *Snowdon from Llyn Nantlle* which is in the Walker Gallery in Liverpool. His canvas, *Caernarvon Castle*, which is in the National Museum of Wales is interesting because it includes an artist sitting in the foreground, drawing in a sketchbook. Perhaps this represents Richard Wilson himself, capturing the beauty of Wales. His work had another effect too, since it helped to dispel the prevailing image of Wales as primitive and barbaric.

But there is another memorial to Richard Wilson, which is passed by hundreds of busy people every day, next door to the estate where he died. There is an inn, for which Wilson once painted the sign in order, it is said, to clear a drinking debt. The inn is called '*We Three Loggerheads*' and it once belonged to the Colomendy Estate. It lies outside Mold on the Ruthin Road, the A494, opposite the entrance to the beautiful Loggerheads Country Park in Denbighshire. The sign swinging in the wind by the side

117

of the busy road is a copy of an original painting by Wilson, a version of which still hangs inside the inn above the stairs. It is a simple uncomplicated cartoon. It allegedly shows the vicar and a local landowner who had been involved in a long – running dispute.

Loggerheads

Originally the word 'loggerhead' meant a stupid person. Thus, the name of a picture displaying only two heads, has been chosen deliberately to involve the viewer as the third stupid person. For an artist who could not find a market for the work about which he felt most deeply, the idea of any viewer of his work as a loggerhead perhaps had a particular appeal.

Footnote

The word was also the name for a tool with a long handle used both for melting pitch and also as a weapon, hence the term 'at loggerheads.' There are three places in the UK with this name and all claim the origins of the phrase 'at loggerheads', meaning a disagreement, as their own.

Monmouth
John Renie 1832

Here Lies John Renie

John Renie's gravestone is odd. There is no other way to describe it. Unless you call it a 'curiosity.' But I am sure you won't have seen anything like it before. It is unique. A square of stone upon which a puzzle has been etched, as if it was a large piece of paper on which someone has tried to amuse themselves for an hour or two. It looks like something a boy would do at the back of a particularly boring Maths lesson.

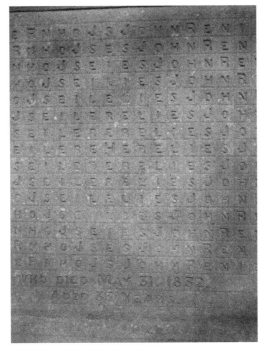

Here Lies John Renie

What it says is nothing more than *'Here lies John Renie.'* A simple sentence, but repeated on the stone apparently 45,760 times. Find the 'H' in the middle of the stone and then head in any direction you want and it will spell out the same thing. *'Here lies John Renie.'* In fact, find any 'H' and you can follow the words in any way you chose. Up, down across, round corners… There are 285 individual letters carved into the stone. 15 down, 19 across. Count them if you want…

Today a computer would design it for us. But John Renie carved it himself. A lasting memorial to an interesting and talented man.

You will find the stone very easily. Just head to the pleasant town of Monmouth and at the top of Monnow Street, above Agincourt Square, you will find St. Mary's Church. If you enter the churchyard where Whitecross Street meets the corner of St. James Square and follow the path up towards the church, you will find John Renie's grave in front of you, on the edge of the path. Alternatively enter the grounds by the Church Street entrance and turn to the right. To be truthful, John Renie isn't there, for the stone was relocated some time ago, but his memorial is there for all to see. It stands alone, with a light-green tinge from the moss. Square and solid and completely peculiar.

John Renie was born in 1799 and became a house painter and glazier, taking over the family business, they say, at the age of thirteen or fourteen and running it from the family home in Monnow Street . He was an intelligent man, though he did not benefit from the level of education that his mind deserved. What is apparent is that he had a sense of duty, both to his family and to his fellow man. He soon developed clearly expressed social principles. He became a founding member of the Oddfellows, one of the many friendly societies that began in the early nineteenth century. Such groups offered support to its members during sickness or injury and pre-dated trade unions and associations. Common humanity and a sense of justice had started to bring people together and they were thoughtful men of belief and conviction.

Renie was a prodigious letter writer to the press, on issues surrounding reform and education. He promoted the idea of skills and craft. In one letter in the *Monmouth Merlin* he writes '*It is possible for a man who has received a classical education to submit to gain his bread by the labour of his hands.*' He goes on to object to the idea that '*too much learning may be considered a dangerous thing for the middling and lower classes of society.*'

At the time, some ascribed John Renie's too-early death to exhaustion. He had worked constantly in support of a radical agenda, supporting the great Reform Act of 1832. He had travelled, speaking repeatedly at public meetings. As a result of his tireless campaigning, the Reform Candidate, 'B. Hall Esq.' was elected in Monmouth. But this triumph didn't bring about his death; sadly it was probably his work that did for him in the end. John Renie's duties for the Oddfellows involved calculating risks connected with the different professions and thus producing actuarial tables. This work must have revealed to him the risks he was facing every day that he worked.

Like so many in our past – and still today - his choice of profession was also the cause of his death. He was poisoned slowly by toxic materials, by the lead in the paints and by the arsenic in the wallpapers. The poisoning even had a name. It was called '*painter's colic.*' From its clutches there was no escape. Death was waiting, patiently.

John Renie was a craftsman, accomplished and thoughtful. His obituary praised him as a man '*of extraordinary natural abilities (who) was impressed with the highest and most romantic enthusiasm for rational liberty.*'

But death did not come upon him quickly, and he had plenty of time to get himself ready. So he chose an idiosyncratic epitaph, each one of the 285 letters chiselled out carefully and precisely.

You wonder what thoughts passed through his mind as each letter was pulled painstakingly from the stone. Such a piece of work.

Some believe that it was designed in order to confuse the Devil. By the time he had worked out what it said, the deceased would have made it to the sanctuary of Heaven.

If this is the case, then we sinners have little to worry about. He might be Lucifer, the fallen angel, but apparently he can't do a word search. But this explanation suggests a level of superstition that, to my mind, is out of keeping with the other things we know about John Renie. As a social reformer and campaigner he would not perhaps have troubled himself too much with the fearful talk of eternal damnation. He might have seen such talk as a means to maintain the status quo. He probably designed his tombstone as he did simply because he could and because of what it meant to him. By creating it, he made his own small mark on history.

St Mary's Church, Monmouth

At the bottom of the stone, in letters that are partly obscured by the grass, there are recorded other members of the family. There is his son John, who died aged 1 in 1823. It also records his wife, Sarah Howells, who died in 1879 and is buried in Fulham, and his eldest son James, named after the grandfather he never met, who died in 1903 in Clapham aged 83.

There are other Renies there too, beneath your feet as you walk through the gate from Church Street. There is John's father, James Renie, who died in 1813 aged 39 and in so doing precipitated John into the family business. There is his sister Frances, who died in February 1821 aged 19 and Robert, his brother, who died in April 1821 aged 20. It was the mother Ann, who outlived them all, dying at 59 in 1835.

And for me, when you stop to think about all these premature deaths, you can possibly begin to see why it was that John Renie designed what he did. It was a hard life and John's immediate family, rather like himself, had a habit of dying young. His father, his younger brother and sister. Then his baby son. Perhaps this is why he sought some kind of lasting memorial. Too many of those around him departed far too quickly. Perhaps he sacrificed the little time he had left in order to create a satisfying pattern, something that he himself would have enjoyed. In this way he could impose a sense of order on a disordered world, one in which those you loved died young, with so much unachieved. Who can say? But for me, there is a sadness behind the quirkiness of that design.

There is something else too, possibly the spookiest thing of all. He died on the 31 May 1832 at the age of 33. A coincidence? For a man clearly interested in puzzles? Was there some sinister design? Look again.

31, 32, 33.

Or was it possibly a deliberate choice? The final proof that life really could be rationally shaped and ordered? Another unanswered question. Certainly his family were left destitute and an appeal was launched to raise money for them and eventually his business was taken over. But what he left behind marks his short life in such a remarkable and unique way.

Oh yes, and quite by chance these two photographs in the book are numbers 32 and 33. Spooky, eh? Count them, if you want …

Montgomery, Powys
John Davies 1821

The Robber's Grave

We were in Montgomery to relax. The smallest county town in England or Wales. It is a beautiful market town with such a fine range of distinguished buildings, that were glowing in the warm sunshine. It is a peaceful place with a romantically ruined castle high above the town, the beautiful church of St Nicholas, and a wonderful town square. It is a lovely place, without motorway or railway. It is a place to make contact with the past and with one story in particular, for it was here in 1821 that John Davies was brought to die.

He was hanged in front of the gaol. A miscarriage of justice if ever there was one. His grave is signposted off the path that leads from the north gate of the churchyard to the church tower. It is marked by a simple wooden cross and it tells such a tale. It speaks of a cursed conspiracy, innocence and perhaps divine outrage. There are some who say that John Davies was a sheep stealer, but the contemporary records are quite clear. He was executed for highway robbery and now lies within The Robber's Grave, where the grass would not grow for a hundred years.

John Davies was, in fact, a slater from Wrexham and circumstances took him to Oakfield Farm near Oswestry, which belonged to Widow Morris. The farm was in a poor condition, for her husband James had been *'an indolent and somewhat dissipated man,'* as an article written in 1860 tells us, and the farm consequently had fallen into neglect. Widow Morris and her daughter, Jane, were struggling to maintain the place on their own. Davies started to help them. And he worked hard, a proper gentleman, attending church and restoring the farm, devoting himself *'exclusively to the interests of his employer.'* He was the perfect stranger, appearing suddenly and changing lives. It is said that he made the farm successful through *'his assiduity and skill.'*

The Robber's Grave

He was there for two years and *'the widow began to regard him more as a friend and a benefactor than a servant; and was not sorry to observe her daughter's growing affection for him, which appeared to be reciprocal.'*

However, he also made enemies.

In the first place, there was Thomas Pearce who had been hopeful of buying the run-down farm at a knock-down price. His cunning investment plans had suddenly been thwarted by Davies. And then there was Robert Parker, who was engaged to be married to Jane Morris. His problem was that Jane and John had fallen in love and she soon renounced her agreement with Parker.

Here, suddenly, were two locally respected men who had reason to remove the influence of the very inconvenient John Davies; two men who became united in a conspiracy to frame him for a robbery he did not commit.

Davies was delayed late on farm business in Welshpool on 19 April 1821 and set off to walk home in the evening but never arrived, for he was arrested for highway robbery, *'accompanied with violence.'* He was accused by William Jones, a labourer employed by Mr Pugh in Wernllwyd, of stealing a watch and coins to the value of £4 12s. 1d. There were no witnesses to the assault and the accusation rested almost entirely upon the evidence of two witnesses, who claimed that they were there when the watch and money were found upon John Davies' person. And, of course, these two men were Pearce and Parker.

Davies vehemently protested his innocence and conducted his own defence in court at the beginning of September 1821. But he had no witnesses who he could call upon and his not guilty plea was rejected. A jury looked the stranger in the eye, listened to the testimony of two respected local men and found Davies guilty. Highway robbery was a capital offence. It wasn't the romantic adventure it is often presented as today. It was terrifying and brutal and so *'sentence of death was passed upon him.'*

At this point Davies spoke eloquently to the court.

The witnesses are men of respectability, and their evidence has appeared plain and conclusive, and my most solemn protestations of innocence could avail me nothing… upon such evidence the jury could pronounce no other verdict. I blame them not. From my soul, too, I forgive those men, upon whose false testimony I have been convicted. But, my lord, I protest most solemnly, before this court, before your lordship, and, above all, before that God in whose presence I must shortly appear, I am entirely guiltless of the crime for which I am about to suffer.

He was especially concerned about Widow Morris and Jane. His greatest wish is to reassure them that they have not been deceived; he has always been the man they believed that he was.

I devoutly hope that my good mistress, and her kind and excellent daughter, may yet be convinced that they have not nourished and befriended a highway robber. I have, therefore, in humble devotion, offered a prayer to Heaven, and I believe it has been heard and accepted. I venture to assert that if I am innocent of the crime for which I suffer, the grass, for one generation at least, will not cover my grave.

He continued to protest his innocence right up until the moment of his death. For contemporaries this was a significant detail. A confession was part of a condemned man's salvation, a way of repaying a debt to society by becoming a warning to others. True repentance was a preparation for salvation; it would give you a fighting chance in the afterlife. But John Davies' continued expression of innocence made people uneasy. Why would he risk eternal damnation when his own death was inevitable anyway? Dying words had always been regarded as carrying with them the power of truth.

He was executed on 14 September 1821. John Davies *'suffered between 12 and 1 o'clock on a drop erected in front of the gaol at Montgomery.'*

At the moment of his execution there was a huge thunderstorm – torrential rain, forked lightning. A moment of Biblical intensity and a clear indication of divine displeasure at the death of an innocent man. Spectators cried out *'The end of all things is come!'* Proof of his innocence if you wish to believe such things, but too late to save John Davies. And lest you believe that this is a mere fantasy, let me assure you that this very localised storm was documented in the weather reports in the contemporary press.

And what of Pearce and Parker, who lied to ensure that an innocent man was hanged in a thunderstorm? Soon Pearce, *'a drinking and blaspheming man,'* died in a blasting accident in a limestone quarry. Parker, once a figure of health and vigour, died of that favourite nineteenth century ailment, the mysterious *'wasting disease.'*

129

They say that the grave stubbornly rejected any grass for a hundred years. In 1851 the graveyard was remodelled and reseeded, but still the grass stubbornly refused to grow.

Numerous attempts have from time to time been made by some who are still alive, and others who have passed away, to bring grass upon that bare spot. Fresh soil had been frequently spread upon it, and seeds of various kinds have been sown, but not a blade had there ever been known to spring from them

People have always been fascinated by the story. However, an early account from 1852 changed the names of those involved. The unnecessary alteration of John's surname from Davies to Newton has caused confusion and unnecessary excitement amongst family historians for years. But John Davies he was. He came from Wrexham and he was hanged for something he didn't do.

The grave is very easy to find, for its notoriety means that it is well signposted. You cannot miss the church in the middle of Montgomery, named after St Nicholas, the patron saint of thieves. Follow the main path and you will see a simple wooden cross marked by a rose bush, an effective contrast to the angled stones that surround it. There is no name. Just the words 'Robber's Grave.' It is simple and effective and yes, the grass does grow now, in a patchy sort of way.

Perhaps we should be pleased. Perhaps it shows that now his soul is finally at rest.

.

Mynachlog-Ddu, Pembrokeshire
Thomas Rees 1876

Big Rebecca

Near Mynachlog-Ddu, in the Preseli Hills above the village, you will find the source of the bluestones used in the construction of Stonehenge. Quite a claim to fame, you might think. But it was a different kind of stone that drew us to the quiet beauty of the village on a sunny day in spring.

It is an unusual stone too, waiting for us in the cemetery at the Bethel Chapel. It is the grave of Thomas Rees and the inscription, in Welsh, reads

No one but God knows
What may happen in a day.
While fetching a cabbage for my dinner
Death came into my garden and struck me.

It is the sort of thing that can really mess up your day.

Twm Carnabwth - a victim of the cabbage harvest

The Preseli hills are always worth a journey and this grave is notable, not only as a record of an unfortunate gardening incident, but also as the resting place of the man at the heart of the first recorded Rebecca Riot, when the newly erected toll gate on what is now the A478 in Efailwen, on the edge of Carmarthenshire and Pembrokeshire, was attacked by men disguised with petticoats and bonnets on 13 May 1839.

The road was used for carting lime, essential for farmers struggling to maintain the fertility of the fields. The imposition of tolls was regarded as an arbitrary tax on the already difficult lives of country people. But the Toll Harvest was a profitable business, more profitable than farming, and requiring little more investment than a gate and a grumpy pensioner with a bag in which to collect the coins. So, since their pensioner could still be considered to be operational, The Whitland Turnpike Trust replaced the gate that had been pulled down. It remained in place for about two weeks before it was destroyed again. At this point the Trust sensibly reconsidered its position and removed it.

This was the very first incident in a serious insurrection that lasted for four years. In this instance the protesters triumphed, but it was a fleeting moment of success. The resentment simmered on, so that very soon there was the dangerous scent of serious insurrection in the air of Wales.

Rebecca was born out of rural desperation. The starting point was what was perceived as a tax on rural life through the tolls that were charged for moving along the roads. The state of those roads was especially poor and the gates run by private trusts collected tolls which were intended to improve standards by reinvesting income in a maintenance programme. But it didn't work. The trusts were, inevitably, profit-making and, as such, bred enormous resentment. The roads did not appear to improve at all and the income the tolls generated seemed to make the poor much poorer and the rich people richer. For example, there were eleven toll gates between Pontarddulais and Carmarthen and a toll had to be paid at each one. Trusts then began to put additional bars across other routes to catch country people on their way to market.

There were other, deeper, tensions too. Rebecca was also about the fear that an ancient way of life was coming to an end. Cheap food imports were destroying the domestic market, putting livelihoods and families at risk. The population had already started to drift towards the towns in a desperate search for employment. The toll gates became an easily identifiable symbol of the neglect that was undermining a traditional way of life.

The Rebecca Riots re-ignited with an attack on the gate at Pwll-Trap and the insurrection quickly spread throughout south-west Wales. A man dressed as a woman acted as the Rebecca and his followers – The Daughters of Rebecca – pulled down gates and smashed toll houses before disappearing into the night.

Suddenly Wales was on the edge of rebellion, even though taking part in the riots was a dangerous thing to do, for to challenge authority in this way could lead to execution or transportation. But an impoverished Welsh-speaking community, paying huge rents to absent English landlords, felt they had no option. They went to their own chapel but paid tithes (generally one tenth of their income) to support the Church of England, which they did not attend. The toll gates were highly visible symbols of all this simmering anger and resentment.

The toll keepers could only charge travellers for one journey per day and so people would gather at midnight to save money by giving themselves every chance of returning within the same day. Angry people at midnight, handing over money and resenting it, was a certain guarantee of inflammatory nights. Gates across the country were destroyed and troops were deployed to suppress the riots. There was an air of disorder and intimidation, with men forced to take part and with others turning up to watch the entertaining humiliation of someone who kept taking money from them. And the mood soon changed, with the rioters less affable and increasingly violent. A gate keeper in Cardiganshire was blinded; one in Swansea was attacked with an iron bar. It was in Pontarddulais that the insurrection reached a tragic climax, when Rebecca and the authorities finally confronted each other in September 1843.

The increasing violence of the protests meant that sympathy had already started to ebb. Secrecy for their protests could no longer be guaranteed and on this occasion the important element of surprise was lost. An informer told the authorities of a planned attack on the Hendy and Pontarddulais gates and armed troops were waiting for the rioters. Gunfire was exchanged, rioters were shot and apprehended. But Rebecca wanted revenge and so two nights later an attack was launched on the unprotected Hendy gate.

The gate keeper there was Sarah Williams who was not just an experienced collector of tolls, but also deeply unpopular. She had been deliberately stationed there by the trust to increase revenue since, unlike some others in her profession, she never let anyone pass without paying. And so this was pay-back time. Her possessions were removed from the gate house by the rioters, who then set fire to the roof. And in the excitable gunfire that surrounded such an attack, Sarah was shot and killed. Was it deliberate? It was more likely to have been accidental. But there was a sense that enough was enough. Riots and disorder were one thing, but the death of an old lady was something else. The attacks faded away.

Some rioters were transported and the disturbances faded away. A Royal Commission was established and legislation was introduced. Unnecessary gates were removed and tolls were reduced, which for some was a success and justified this popular uprising. But it is clear now that the accelerating decline of the rural economy could not be reversed. Nothing could prevent the inevitable triumph of industrialisation that would change their world forever. Rebecca won the battle, but in the long run lost the war.

And what of our gardener, Thomas Rees from Mynachlog-Ddu, who was known as Twm Carnabwth, named after the house where he lived? He was a radical agricultural labourer who appears to have escaped unpunished after his part in the original attack in Efailwen. He later became a prize fighter until he lost an eye in a brawl. With his one eye, he finally saw the Light and turned towards the path of righteousness by becoming an elder of Bethel chapel, until he was suddenly called to greater things in his garden. You can find him easily, at the back of the cemetery, on the right.

There is another interesting gravestone associated with the riots, for the shadow of Rebecca can still be found in the strangest places. It is up against the wall of the Holy Trinity Church in Newcastle Emlyn. It is the grave of John Kearns, a member of the Light Dragoons who was based in Carmarthen. During the disturbances in June 1843 he was drowned whilst swimming, off duty, in the river. You should see it before it disappears forever, for there is such a danger that we might lose it. The inscription on his fading gravestone tells us

He fell not in the battle strife, nor on the sultry plain.
Death did not meet the warrior there, nor on the storm main.
But there, in Tivy's winding stream, one sunny summer's day,
Where bathing peacefully he sank, his spirit passed away.

And so finally where did the idea of Rebecca come from?

There are a number of explanations. It could have been taken from a quotation in Genesis, *"And they blessed Rebecca and said unto her, let thy seed possess the gates of those which hate them."* A church-going population would have seen the reference instantly. Alternatively, it represented a symbolic inversion of the natural order of things, with women taking action, not men, and with men wearing women's clothes, a symbol of their own world which had gone mad. Or perhaps it was simply that the very first, Twm Carnabwth, disguised himself by borrowing a dress from a neighbour from Llangolman who was called "Rebecca Fawr" (Big Rebecca.).

135

Like you, that is the explanation that I prefer.

At the Holy Trinity Church, Newcastle Emlyn

Newport
Perce Blackborow 1949

Time from start to finish 55 minutes.

This is a story of the eventful life of a modest man. And a cat. It is a story of the sea, of stowaways, of adventure - and of a final sardine.

Perce Blackborow in St Woolos' Cemetery, Newport

Perce Blackborow was born in Newport in April 1894 to a sea-going family. His father, John, was a ship's steward and clearly he wished to follow the family vocation. He was so keen that he originally added a year to his age, as often happened, so that he could go to sea.

One of his earliest engagements was spent serving as a deck hand on a London registered ship, the *Ladywood* from which he was discharged in 1912. The next record of him is on the ship *Golden Gate,* which was wrecked at Montevideo in 1914, leaving Perce and a couple of friends stranded in South America. They travelled to Buenos Aires in search of a new ship.

The polar explorer, Ernest Shackleton, had left London on 1 August 1914, heading for Antarctica in the *Endurance.* The object of the expedition was to cross the Antarctic from one side to the other, via the South Pole. He also put into Buenos Aires, where he immediately sacked three of the crew, thus creating welcome employment opportunities. The two friends were taken on as Able Seamen, but the inexperienced Perce was not. However, those friends smuggled him on board and hid him in a locker, bringing him food as often as they could. This has subsequently given Perce Blackborow legendary status, as the only man ever to have stowed away on an expedition to the extreme weather of the Antarctic.

When Perce was eventually discovered, after three days in a locker, he had been so cramped that he couldn't stand, and Shackleton had to put him in a chair to interview him. It was a very heated interview and it ended with the Boss, as he was called, saying to Perce, *'Do you know that on these expeditions we often get very hungry and, if there is a stowaway available, he is the first to be eaten?'* Perce's response was to say *'They'd get a lot more meat off you, sir,'* and Shackleton sent him off to join the cook as a steward. Frankly, there was not much else he could do, other than throw him overboard, and even in those days that was largely frowned upon.

Blackborow became a proper member of the crew and was accepted happily by his colleagues as they sailed into the south. He formed a particularly close relationship with the ship's cat, Mrs Chippy, although he was, in fact, a boy. Let me explain.

The ship's carpenter, Henry McNeish, brought his cat with him on the expedition. The cat was a useful addition to the crew, since

138

he was a very good mouser and ratcatcher. He was particularly devoted to his master and the cat followed McNeish, the ship's chippy or carpenter, around with such devotion that he was called Mrs. Chippy, even though he was a tomcat. Perce was honoured to be accepted as Mrs Chippy's second-best friend.

At one point, the cat jumped out of a porthole into the cold waters of the South Atlantic but fortunately it was a quiet night and the cat's cries were heard, so the ship turned around to rescue him. Mrs Chippy survived his ten minutes in the sea, but it was as if the poor cat had a premonition that things were not going to go very well, for Shackleton's expedition was ill-starred. He had been involved in polar exploration for some time and was familiar with the extreme conditions that he would face, but Shackleton's expedition sailed into the pack ice a few days before it had been expected. They struggled through for about 400 miles (at a rate of 1 mile per hour) and found clear water in front of the Great Barrier, a huge wall of ice, before becoming irrevocably stuck in January 1915. They were unable to escape from the clutches of the ice.

They had no alternative but to wait. But the bitter winter set in and the *Endurance* was trapped forever. The crew showed patience and passed their time in seal hunting for meat and playing football on the ice. Blackborow, as assistant to the cook, prepared food on a stove that was heated by burning seal or penguin blubber, which was a very smelly fuel and extremely smoky, with the capacity to block out the light. But in April, the light disappeared more permanently, for the polar night began, with the sun disappearing for 10 weeks.

It was tedious and frighteningly cold. Blackborow would later describe Antarctica as 'that barren land of mystery,' but it was also very threatening and inhospitable. It seemed determined to destroy them. The pressure from the ice increased until 27 October, when *Endurance* could endure no more and was finally crushed. *Endurance* was abandoned, with the nearest land 350 miles away. They decided to walk there across the ice, dragging their lifeboats with them, and all on a ration of eight ounces of food a day. And in these extreme circumstances, there was no space for passengers.

Whilst he was fed and warm, Mrs. Chippy had few concerns, although he wasn't too fussed about penguin meat. But to some, he could become a liability. Most of the crew were very fond of him. The cat probably represented a contact with domestic normality in the frozen and alien environment in which they found themselves. Indeed, the doctor said, *'Mrs. Chippy's almost total disregard for the diabolical forces at work on the ship was more than remarkable – it was inspirational. Such perfect courage is, alas, not to be found in our modern age.'* However, such eulogies did not save him. When the decision was taken to walk away from the wreck, there was no place for Mrs Chippy. He was to be left behind. Survival had to come before sentiment.

Sad goodbyes were said and Perce, from somewhere, produced a tin of sardines, Mrs Chippy's favourite. The condemned cat ate a hearty meal, then the poor thing was shot. It was a tough life as a ship's cat.

McNeish never forgave Shackleton for this and harboured a resentment for the rest of his life. He did his very best to prepare the lifeboats for their epic journey, but he became increasingly difficult, to the extent that he was not recommended by Shackleton for the award of a polar medal.

But their march across the ice was not a success and they abandoned the attempt after three days. The surface of the ice was just too uneven. They established what they called 'Ocean Camp' and waited until December, when they tried again. They covered eight miles in nine days but were forced to give up once again. Their new camp was called 'Patience Camp.'

The advantage of camping on ice-flows, of course, is that they move, and by March 1916, they were 100 miles from land. The ice was starting to break up around them and as soon as they had clear water they launched their boats. In April, they managed to land on Elephant Island in the south Shetlands. The honour of being the first man ashore was given to Blackborow, the youngest member of the expedition. Solid land for the first time in 16 months.

He had suffered very badly from frostbite on both feet and when they helped him over the side of the boat, he collapsed in the surf and did not move. He had to be helped to the shore.

Here the party divided. Shackleton and five others set out for South Georgia in search of rescue, leaving the sick and weak behind. There was considerable anxiety about the state of some of the men, for they had lived in a state of semi-starvation for a considerable time. They camped underneath the overturned lifeboats and waited. The greatest concerns were for Blackborow, for soon he contracted gangrene.

On 15 June, all the toes on his left foot were amputated, with insufficient instruments and with only a blubber stove to keep the temperature above freezing. The surgeon, Greenstreet, said, '*the poor beggar behaved splendidly and it went without a hitch. Time from start to finish 55 minutes.*' Such is the fate of a stowaway. They were marooned on Elephant Island for almost 5 months. When Shackleton eventually returned in August, Perce was carried to a high rock so he could finally see their rescue. And Shackleton's proudest boast that he had never lost a man was kept intact.

Perce was a modest man and made little of his adventures in Antarctica. He spent three months in hospital in Punta Arenas in Chile before returning home. He was so embarrassed at the welcome party awaiting him at Newport Station, that he crossed the tracks and found an alternative exit. Indeed, it is said that he mentioned nothing to his bride, Kate, about his missing toes until his wedding night.

He worked as a boatman in Alexandra Docks in Newport, rarely speaking of his formative and dramatic experiences. He was awarded the Bronze Polar Medal for his part in the ill-fated expedition. He died of bronchitis and heart disease in 1949, aged 54.

You will find Perce deep within the extensive St. Woolos Cemetery in Newport. Drive in through the gates on Basseleg Road and then follow the lanes to the left for about 300 yards and then turn right into Section CON D30. Half way along on the right hand side, opposite a bench, you will find the fine black and shiny headstone facing away from you. Here Perce lies with his wife Kate and two of their six children, Jack and Philip, who died in infancy.

An interesting postscript to the story is provided by the carpenter McNeish, who went to live in New Zealand. His achievements were marked in 2004, when a bronze sculpture of Mrs Chippy was added to his restored grave in Karori Cemetery in Wellington. Cat and master properly honoured, Mrs Chippy not forgotten.

You suspect that Perce would have been pleased.

Newtown, Powys
Sir Pryce Pryce-Jones 1920

The Man who Taught the World to Shop

They are such wonderful buildings and they dominate Newtown in Powys. Two tall, distinctive, sturdy red brick temples to commerce. The Royal Welsh Warehouse.

The story behind the buildings is one that has touched all our lives. It is a story of an entrepreneur who transformed his town, transformed his own life, transformed the world and built the future. This is the story of Sir Pryce Pryce-Jones.

Pryce Jones, Newtown

Pryce Jones, as he was christened in 1834, was apprenticed at the age of 12 to a draper, John Davies on the Cross in Newtown. He soon discovered that it was a profession that suited him. In 1859, when he was 25, he opened his own small shop, just off Broad Street and traded under his own name.

It was from here in Newtown that he changed forever the shopping experience of the world. He developed a mail order business, beginning in a small way by sending out patterns and stock lists. He was a man who knew his market intimately and also knew that there was an untapped market out there in isolated rural locations like mid Wales, where shops were sometimes occasional.

Jones went on to link distribution to production, by arranging for local woollen manufacturers and merchants to supply goods to fulfil the orders he received, rather than holding a large amount of stock. A simple idea, but revolutionary.

He was always eager to extend the business and he discovered that he had a gift for publicity. In 1862, he received an order from Florence Nightingale and immediately began using her name as an endorsement. Queen Victoria and members of European royalty– The Empress of Austria, The Queens of Denmark and of Naples - soon became his customers. In capital letters across the bottom of one of his leaflets, he proudly boasted that his company was the

MAKER OF THE EMBROIDERED PETTICOAT
PRESENTED TO HER ROYAL HIGHNESS THE
PRINCESS OF WALES.

But one product more than any other, came to define his business. A rug.

The Euklisia rug was exported around the world. Really, it was a combination of rug, shawl and inflatable pillow. In fact, it was the very first prototype of the sleeping bag, very popular in the German army during the Franco-Prussian war. It consisted of a woollen blanket with a pocket at the top for an inflatable,

144

vulcanised rubber pillow. You folded the blanket over and fastened it together. It was exported all over the world to places like the Congo and the Australian outback although, sadly, no examples survive.

Pryce Jones had a contract to provide 60,000 rugs to the Russian army, to be supplied at the rate of 6,000 rugs each week. They were used during the Russo-Turkish War at the siege of Plevna in 1877. However, when the city fell, the Russians cancelled the rest of their order, leaving Jones with 17,000 undelivered rugs. He quickly added the Euklisia Rug to his catalogue and sold it as inexpensive bedding for charities working with the poor.

Pryce Jones has the honour of calling the special attention of Ladies to the following. He has on hand seventeen thousand Brown Army Blankets (fitted with an air tight pillow) which were expressly made for the Russian Army. … P.J. proposes to clear off the lot at a great sacrifice - he intends removing the air tight pillows and sewing up the slot, the space may, if required, be refilled with a pillow of feathers, wool, cotton or straw, and may in this manner, be utilized for the poor - being a bed and blanket combined. As P.J. offers these goods under cost of production, he solicits and hopes to receive early orders.

I am sure that selling these books of mine would not have been a problem for him at all.

In 1879 Jones built new spacious premises. The Royal Welsh Warehouse, which we can still see today, was deliberately sited next to the station. The London and North Western Railway Company would soon provide three dedicated parcel wagons to carry packages for Pryce Jones, which were dropped off at Shrewsbury, Stafford, Rugby, Willesden and Euston. At these stations, connections with other lines ensured that an order could reach almost every part of England the following day. Soon he was receiving 2,000 orders every day and he built a second warehouse, Agriculture House, connected to the first by a bridge.

The entrance

In 1882, while Jones was campaigning to become Conservative MP for the Montgomery Boroughs, he met the Postmaster General and suggested to him the idea of developing a parcel service. A letter post already existed, but parcels had to be sent by road and rail carriers, sometimes at great expense - obviously an important consideration for a mail order operation. His idea was adopted and the parcel post was developed as a result. The Royal Welsh Warehouse acquired its own printing press and in 1890 produced its first illustrated catalogue to replace the simple price lists that had been sent out previously. In 1901 he added his own post office to the Royal Welsh Warehouse, to manage the huge number of packages sent all over the world from Newtown.

He was knighted in 1887 for his services to commerce and he expanded his name, rather as he had expanded his business, to become Sir Pryce Pryce-Jones. He served as MP from 1885 to 1886, but for many he was never anything other than a draper's assistant and as a politician he was, to some, a figure of fun. He became High Sheriff for Montgomeryshire in 1891 but as a Conservative he faced hostility from local Liberals. In 1892 he visited Llanidloes and there were disturbances. Stones were thrown. There were scuffles as he approached his train. He continued to brandish his walking stick about in an angry way, and inadvertently struck a little girl just above the eye and caused a wound which began to bleed. The enraged crowd became extremely hostile, his hat was taken and then marched through the streets on a clothes prop and then burnt.

But politics is not what he is remembered for. He was a man who went from shop assistant to multi-millionaire, responsible for 4,000 workers and 250,000 customers. Those two towering buildings symbolise his huge achievements.

When we visited it seemed rather forlorn . The beautiful panels showing the cities where their products were exhibited are clean and bright and above the door there are panels showing ships and trains. But it's time has gone.

Inside there are ornate features, a marvellous staircase, handrails, stained glass windows. None of this is necessary at all. But it reflects pride in achievement, the idea that commerce can be proud and elegant. Agriculture House has a completely unnecessary but lovely wind vane.

There were still businesses within the building, struggling valiantly, but it was very silent place, with an air of desperation.

There have been attempts to keep it alive as the Pryce Jones Retail Centre. But whilst it is still directly outside the train station, it is separated from the main part of the town by the busy A489 and you need a compelling reason to cross it. Unless a big name retail store moves in, the building will forever be on the wrong side of the road. The world has moved on and often most of it seems to be moving on the A489.

Pryce Jones died in 1920 at the age of 85, when his business was still reasonably intact. It suffered, like everyone, in the Great Depression and was eventually taken over by another mail order business. But Pryce Jones made a huge contribution to Newtown in his lifetime by reviving the local woollen industry. He pioneered new methods of trading which are now taken for granted. What he created became a global phenomenon and a way of life.

His resting place acknowledges none of this. It is marked by a distinguished obelisk on the right hand side in the grounds of All Saints Church in Llanllwchaiarn, that he built on the other side of the river Severn. If you didn't know you would say that this was the grave of some forgotten local worthy. But it is the resting place of a man with an extraordinary story, a man who changed the world.

The grave of Pryce Pryce-Jones

Pantteg, Neath
The Murder of Morgan Lewis 1850

I will serve Morgan Lewis before he sleeps

The earth moves in Pantteg. In December 2012 thousands of tons of mud slid down the hill, following prolonged and heavy rain. Homes were vulnerable, residents were evacuated. Trees, their roots released, had sailed inexorably downhill on a piste of mud to rest against the vestry and the cemetery wall. It happened again in 2017 and it has been on the move before – in 1965 – and it will surely happen again. That is why Mynydd Allt y Grug is known as The Moving Mountain.

The grave is centre left, with the shaped stone resting on it

And when it does happen again, we may lose one of our secret treasures, for the cemetery contains a fascinating gravestone. Of course, it has no value in itself. It is a simple thing, just a damaged gravestone, cracked and weather-worn, but the story it tells, the window it opens into the past, makes it irreplaceable, even if it tells a sadly all too-familiar story.

Men drinking; men arguing; men fighting.

Morgan Lewis lived in Graigarw (now Pantteg) on the hillside near Ystalyfera. He was a powerfully built man, married to Rachel, the father of six daughters and an extremely unpopular man in the area. As the local paper, the *Cambrian,* reported, Morgan was '*not considered, on many accounts, a favourite in the place.*' This was, to some extent, a consequence of his profession. He was under-gamekeeper for the local worthy, Mr R. D. Gough. This marked him out as a class traitor, standing between the working man who became a poacher out of necessity, as the only way he could feed his hungry family.

Of course, it was never so straightforward. Landowners believed that the romantic notion of the poacher was often some considerable distance from the truth. For them, it wasn't about survival at all, but about profit, with stolen game sold to dealers in pubs for beer money. Nonetheless, someone like Morgan Lewis was seen to be protecting a leisure pursuit, at the expense of the needs of his own community.

And so it was that he was killed by a notorious local poacher, 23 year old David Davies from Llanguicke, who worked in the local tinworks. He also had a well-established reputation, though so far he had escaped any conviction for poaching.

The cause of their dispute on Friday 22 February 1850 we will never know. It began at about 6.00pm at the Wern Fawr Public House. The two men had been drinking together. They were acquaintances, indeed Davies had recently called on the family to inquire after one of the daughters, who had been unwell. But their friendship was always a fragile one and their conversation turned into an argument. Words were exchanged. *'Insulting language'* was used. Witnesses said that it was Davies who struck the first blow. Outside the pub, Lewis, the older man and the stronger man, gave Davies a considerable beating. He hit him round the head, grabbed him by the hair, knocked him down into the gutter and kicked him repeatedly. Others intervened, concerned that he might kill him, such was the ferocity of the assault. Davies went away to wash his face in a local brook, where, perhaps, he picked up a rock. He then told his brothers, John and Jenkin, *'I will serve Morgan Lewis before he sleeps.'*

Lewis returned to Pantteg and called into the Miner's Arms. Soon Rachel came to find her husband. She'd heard that Davies was telling everyone that he intended to kill him and so arrived to take Morgan home.

Davies suddenly appeared. He was shouting loudly that Lewis had caught him poaching but that Davies had paid him off. He had a stone concealed behind his back. It was a large stone, weighing perhaps one and a half pounds and he hurled it at Lewis from a distance of about 2 yards. It struck him on the forehead, just above the left eye. He caught the stone as he fell to the ground, bleeding *'like a pig.'* He pulled himself up, boasting that despite his best efforts, Davies had failed – he still lived. In reply, Davies threw a second stone at Rachel but missed. He ran away.

Morgan was taken home to bed. When the doctor came on Saturday, he found a cut on his forehead which *'extended in depth to the bone.'* He seemed to be fine but, of course, you can never tell with head wounds. And, whilst his recovery seemed to be progressing, on Sunday there was a crisis within the skull. By midnight he was unconscious and he died on Monday. An examination showed that he had *'a fractured skull and inflammation of the brain.'*

Davies was desperately packing, getting ready to flee, when he was arrested by Superintendent Vigors, to whom Rachel handed over the stone that had killed her husband. There was still blood and skin on it.

He was tried for manslaughter and assault. Of course, anything less than murder would never satisfy the family, but there was felt to be sufficient provocation by Lewis for Davies to escape that accusation. Lewis had over-reacted to Davies; he was the one who had escalated the argument. There was considerable local sympathy for Davies. The *Cambrian* reported that '*The inquest was besieged by the people of the place, and the greatest sympathy was shown for the prisoner. We cannot say the same for the poor widow.*'

When it came to court a week later in March, the proceedings were over very quickly. Davies was found guilty of manslaughter – there really was no alternative – but with a recommendation to mercy. He was sentenced to 3 months imprisonment with hard labour.

All that was left to the Lewis family was the anger that drove them to make a permanent statement on a gravestone. They had seen the law in action, but had found no justice they could understand. The inscription states clearly that Lewis had been killed by Davies, with two boldly engraved fingers pointing at the name.

This stone was erected
To the memory of
Morgan Lewis of Graigarw in this Parish
Who died February 25th 1850
Aged 38 years
Having received a fatal blow with a stone at the hand of
David Davies

Then, there is a verse, translated from the Welsh.

Here is the resting place of Morgan, struck
By a stone to the head:
By mishap, this dreadful thing befell him
Take care and remember all this.

At the top of the grave there is a carved stone to represent the one he threw. Some say that it is in fact the original stone. They also say that it was regularly painted red.

Notice that David Davies' name is larger than that of Morgan Lewis

The gravestone now is badly cracked. It stands forlorn in the uneven ground. Not worth a second glance, until you know the story that it carries. Let us remember the story before the earth moves again and takes it back forever. Because whilst the community might one day be betrayed once again by the land, back in 1850 a family felt betrayed by the law.

153

Rhos, Conwy
Harold Lowe 1944

The water's freezing and there are not enough boats

In June 1912 there was a reception for him back in Wales, at the Barmouth Picture Pavilion, and over 1000 people attended. Here he was presented with gifts of nautical equipment from grateful survivors. They were inscribed '*To Harold Godfrey Lowe, 5ᵗʰ Officer RMS Titanic. The real hero of the Titanic. With deepest gratitude.*' Harold Lowe found a place in history. And he was born and he died in Wales.

The white-washed Llandrillo church in Rhos

He was born in November 1882 in Llandrillo yn Rhos and spent his childhood in Barmouth, learning to sail on the Mawddach estuary. When he was fourteen, he objected to his father's suggestion that he should take up an apprenticeship. *'I was not going to work for anybody for nothing.'* So off he went to sea. An impetuous decision perhaps, but also a momentous one, which ultimately saved lives and got him a part in a Hollywood blockbuster.

Lowe ended up spending five years working along the west coast of Africa before he joined the White Star Line. He worked his way up the ranks, studying for certificates for Second Mate, through to Master Mariner. He served as Third Officer on a couple of their other liners crossing the Atlantic. before he was assigned to the *Titanic* in March 1912. *'The largest, safest and most luxurious ship in the world.'* A great honour. The start of a glittering career. And he did make his mark, but not in the way he anticipated.

Lowe was one of the officers who tested two lifeboats to fulfil Board of Trade requirements before it left Southampton. But because it was truly unsinkable, lifeboat provision was hardly important. In fact, Captain Smith decided not to hold a lifeboat drill to familiarise passengers and crew with procedures at all. There was no need to fuel unnecessary anxieties. But even if the ship did, in fact, exceed the archaic lifeboat requirements for a ship of such size, there were still nowhere near enough.

To begin with everything was entirely routine, as you might expect on a luxury hotel afloat in the Atlantic. Down below however, in third class, there were hundreds of passengers who had never been anywhere near a hotel in their lives.

Lowe got on with his work, unaware of the many ice warnings that were being received. The crew worked four hours on and four hours off, which was a very exhausting shift pattern, giving little time for relaxation and recovery. So, on Sunday 14 April 1912, when he was relieved on his watch at 8.15 pm, he went straight to bed. This would explain why it was, that when the ship hit the fateful iceberg at 11.40 pm, he was fast asleep and oblivious to the impact; oblivious to the transmission of the world's first SOS message; oblivious too, to the fact that the early radio enthusiast, Arthur Moore, was one of the first people to hear it. But there was little that Arthur could do, for he was far away in his home at Gelligroes Mill in Pontllanfraith. They have never launched lifeboats from there.

Contact with a large, solitary iceberg popped rivets and buckled hull plates below the *Titanic's* waterline. From that moment, the great ship was doomed. Fatal design flaws were revealed. Perhaps it was as simple as inadequate rivets. But the absurd and pretentious arrogance of man had been fractured by a lump of ice. To bring a ship like the *Titanic* to the same place as a deadly iceberg deliberately, in the vastness of the Atlantic, would have been as complicated as co-ordinating a moon landing. Yet Nature did it so easily and casually, as Thomas Hardy describes in his poem *The Convergence of the Twain.*

Of course, we know where the *Titanic* is today. It has been filmed and explored. But the iceberg soon melted and disappeared. It is all around us now, perhaps even as a residual memory in the water that you will drink today.

Some people claim that they saw the iceberg. Passengers on the German ship *Prinz Adalbert* saw a jagged, ugly piece of ice with a red scar along the side, large enough on the surface, but with an even greater bulk beneath.

When Lowe eventually emerged from his sleep and made it up on to the deck, there were passengers wearing lifebelts and the lifeboats were being made ready for lowering. It was at this time that they started to realise that there were insufficient berths in the boats for the number of passengers they carried. But then, why should there have been? The *Titanic* was unsinkable, an idea offering little comfort as the great ship began to settle and tilt in

156

the water. Harold could feel it under his feet, the bow moving downwards and, anticipating the imminent chaos around him, he returned to his cabin to collect his revolver.

He started to help passengers into boats, though he was particularly concerned that they were being over-filled and that the boats would thus collapse. Lowe had experience of small boats from his childhood, but many of the other seamen had not. And they had to man and lower twenty boats, without ever having practised the necessary procedures.

It was for this reason that he had an encounter with Bruce Ismay, the managing director of the White Star Line, who was travelling on this inauspicious voyage. He told Ismay to get out of his way, for he had work to do. In fact, he told him to get the hell out of the way.

Lowe knew what he was doing, he knew experienced crew had to take control, and because of this, they lowered Boat 5 with thirty nine people on it. He was then sent over to the other side of the ship to supervise the lowering of Boat 14.

His unrestrained outburst would later endear Lowe to the press, since Ismay was vilified for surviving, when so many others who put their faith in his company did not. Thus, Harold Lowe became a spokesman for so many others when he said what he did. To us, his use of excitable language to his boss is understandable in these circumstances, but it was a shocking transgression to his contemporaries. It became a notorious moment, a key element in the mythology of the sinking, but it was not half as notorious as that moment when Lowe fired his revolver to establish a sense of order.

These were completely unexpected circumstances and Lowe rose to the occasion, taking control and bringing an order that would allow a lucky few to survive. He took responsibility, realising that duty transcended status.

The scene on the decks was peculiar. People were having to deal with the one thing they never felt would happen and in the early stages of the sinking, so many thought it would all be sorted out. It was impossible to think that the cold, dark sea was safer than the huge illuminated liner, this luxurious and elegant triumph of human achievement, a piece of the Empire afloat on the ocean. Of course, the poorer passengers down in steerage, who died in such huge numbers, found it difficult to find their way up to the boat deck, a part of the ship they would not otherwise have visited. In this way, the *Titanic* was a microcosm of Edwardian society and a world that would change forever in 1914, with the outbreak of war. And perhaps the sinking of the *Titanic* played its own part in the erosion of those values. It must be hard to understand social divisions when you are about to drown.

In other sections, passengers wandered around quite aimlessly and boats were released with very few people on them. Boat 1 was launched with only 12 in it, Sir Cosmo and Lady Duff and their maid the most prominent, along with 9 men. It is the boat around which rumours emerged, including the suggestion that the crew were bribed not to return to the site of the sinking to rescue those struggling in the water.

The instruction that it was 'women and children first,' meant that some couples refused to be separated and watched the drama in an almost detached way, arm in arm. With insufficient boats and no ordered way of allocating places, such a random approach to survival was perhaps inevitable. And we all, always, ask ourselves how we would have reacted ourselves. Who can say? But you know, as you read about it all, that Harold Lowe did the right thing.

Nonetheless, in parts of the ship there was a scene of chaos with men, according to the mythology, disguising themselves as women to get a precious place in a lifeboat. These boats were in danger of being overloaded, particularly Boat 14, where passengers tried to force themselves on- board as it was being lowered. Lowe was the officer with responsibility for the boat and so removed

158

one young man who was hiding under a seat and then fired his revolver into the night sky to stop the boat being swamped by desperate men. The tackle for lowering the boat had become jammed and it stopped about 5 feet from the surface. Lowe ordered the ropes to be cut and the lifeboat slapped down into the sea. And whilst they bailed out the boat with their hats, Lowe took them all away from the *Titanic*.

He raised the mast in anticipation of a breeze at dawn. He had developed the skills to sail the lifeboat in his childhood and so was clearly the right man in the right place. Lowe gathered other lifeboats together into a small fleet, tying some of them together for safety. He was completely the man in charge, squashing more survivors into the boats under his control. Whilst the survivors felt they were overcrowded, Lowe knew there was still room.

Other crew members back on board resigned themselves to their fate. They knew well what was happening and knew with equal certainty that their own fate had been decided the moment the ship's hull had been split. They had no role to play. The ship's 'boys' who helped the passengers into the boats, the domestic staff, the band that famously played on until the very end - there were no places for them. They were doomed.

From the comparative safety of their vantage point, Lowe's passengers saw the *Titanic* sink. The stern rose high into the air, the lights went off, came on again and then went out forever. She slid beneath the calm sea. It was 2.20 am, a little over three hours since the collision with the iceberg. And the silence that followed was horribly broken, for those in the lifeboats could hear the terrible cries of people struggling in the freezing water.

Lowe was the only person who took his boat back into the wreckage to see if he could rescue anyone. He made space by distributing passengers into the tethered boats. He was quite brisk in giving instructions, especially as some of the passengers didn't want to risk their own safety by picking up others. *'Jump, damn you!'*

he cried at one woman, as he moved her into another boat. He was accused of blasphemy and drunkenness, which was amused Lowe, for he was an abstainer. But in these extreme circumstances he could perhaps be granted a little latitude.

When he decided it was safe, he rowed back into what remained after the disaster. Some hard choices had to be made. He knew that he could not go back in too soon or he would be swamped by desperate people clinging to the boat in huge numbers. He had to wait for their numbers to diminish. When they eventually went back they were confronted by an awful scene. There were hundreds of bodies, dead from hypothermia, floating in the sea, supported by their lifebelts. They could not row because of the number of corpses. They had to push their way through. They rescued four men, one of whom died quite soon afterwards. And as they retreated from the awful wreckage, they all burst into tears.

As dawn broke he sailed the lifeboat back to others and they waited, ready to be rescued by the *Carpathia*. At the Board of Enquiry he was asked what he did next. He replied, '*There was nothing to do.*' All they could do was wait and stare at the huge expanse of water, under which the *Titanic* had disappeared so quickly. It was an unlikely scene, for the Atlantic had been flat calm throughout the night. It had a dream-like quality. All that suffering and death, chaos and then silence. No trace anywhere of a luxury liner.

Of course, many of the passengers were grateful for what he had done. But he refused any money that was offered to him. '*I will never take money for doing my duty.*'

Lowe himself may have suffered from 'Survivor Guilt,' as he saw so few survive and so many perish. There was a cruel randomness about those who died and those who lived, and he was, by chance, involved in those decisions. He was certainly unprepared for the media interest that surrounded the tragedy and the testimony he was required to give at the enquiries. The *Titanic* was his place in the sun, though in later life he rarely spoke about it at all and he willingly settled back into welcome obscurity. Harold Lowe married Ellen Whitehouse in 1913 and had two children. They were the future; the *Titanic* was behind him.

But he never lost his connection with the sea and spent the rest of his working life on it in some capacity or other. The First World War was spent in the Royal Naval Reserve and the Second World War as an air raid warden. He was a man who understood the concept of duty and such obligations defined him. It is said that, whilst he had the manners of a gentleman, his speech was littered with the language of his life at sea. He had no inhibitions, either on the *Titanic* or in later life.

Lowe kept a boat of his own, long into his retirement. He died of a stroke on 12 May 1944. He was 61.

Much later, he would be played by the Welsh actor Ioan Gruffudd in the famous film, which acknowledges his role in recuing survivors when he rescues the fictional lead, Rose, from the icy sea. In reality, it was a Chinese man called Fang Lang who Lowe found and rescued from a floating door, not a lovelorn heroine.

Lang was one of six Chinese sailors later vilified for their survival, at a time of virulent anti-Chinese sentiment. They were all expelled from America as soon as they had landed, under the Chinese Exclusion Act. Lang did later settle in America but, rather like Lowe, never spoke of his escape from the Titanic to anyone.

If you wish to pay your respects to Harold, you must leave the A55 in North Wales and take the B5115 to Llandudno. As you reach Rhos, the road takes a sharp turn to the right and there at the top of the rise, on the right hand side, you will find Llandrillo church. It is very appropriate, I think, that the church was white-washed to serve as a landmark for sailors at sea.

It took us a while to locate the grave, for it is a large cemetery.

In the end, it was our grandsons, Alex and Will who found him, close up against the boundary wall of the ancient church, next to the road. As befits a modest man of principal, his grave is understated and discreet. It carries no hint at all of the part that he played in one of the defining events of the century.

Devoted Husband
Harold Godfrey Lowe
Com. R. D. R. N. R.

I Thank my God upon
Every Remembrance
Of You.

Harold Lowe, hero of the Titanic

And in some ways it is even more moving when you stop and consider the unacknowledged story that hides behind those words.

St Asaph, Denbighshire
Dic Aberdaron 1843

In Chester, constantly blowing a ram's horn

He was known as Dic Aberdaron and was regarded as eccentric, enigmatic and downright odd. The North Wales Express said of him

Among the singular characters which nature sometimes produces... few have been more remarkable than Richard Robert Jones, of Aberdaron, in Caernarvonshire, who although an excellent linguist, is, in almost every other respect, an idiot.

Harsh words perhaps, but the newspaper had no fear that their victim would object to their assessment, because Dic Aberdaron lived in his own insular and peculiar world.

Richard Robert Jones was born in Morfa Llwyn Glas, about two miles from Aberdaron, at the far end of the Lleyn Peninsular in 1780 and achieved fame – or notoriety - for his unusual facility with languages. Today, we would say that he was a savant, someone with an autistic disorder who displays exceptional ability in one particular area. For Jones, it appears to have been archaic languages, and this inspired a wariness in others, who may probably have believed that he had, in some way, been touched by the Divine.

His father was a carpenter who owned a small cargo boat and shuttled between Wales and Liverpool, but any hopes he may once have had, of passing on the business to his son, were lost in the strange tidal forces of his son's unusual mind. Dic's apprenticeship was an abject failure. He had no practical inclinations at all and found it easy to neglect his duties. His father used to flog him regularly for reading on the boat instead of watching the tiller, but such retribution was futile. Dic had a consuming mania for learning languages. In response, his father, perhaps understandably, regarded him as a waster. Dic's interests, and his inability to engage with the daily obligations of rural working life, clearly exasperated him.

Richard's formal education had always been sporadic and it was not until he was nine years of age that he was able to read the Bible in Welsh. He apparently found it very difficult to learn English, but once he had a basic understanding, the floodgates seemed to open. At the age of 10, Richard began to study Latin, and soon he had acquired Greek, closely followed by Hebrew, Greek, Chaldaic, Arabic, Persian, French and Italian. In the end, without the help of education, Dic Aberadon could converse in thirty five languages, considerably in excess of the number required for daily life in North Wales.

He left home to escape beatings from an exasperated father and spent much of his life in transit, learning more languages. He had a thick beard, a shapeless hat, often wore an old Dragoon's jacket, and travelled the country with his books and a succession of stray cats, wandering from country house to parsonage, looking for support and arguing with inn keepers who were foolish enough to give him lodgings. He always carried with him a large number of books which he decorated with prints of cats cut from old ballad sheets.

Sometimes he had to sell books to buy food, but he would always try to buy them back with any money he received. On one occasion, he had to part with a precious Hebrew Bible which he was subsequently unable to recover, so in 1807 he went to London to buy another. He ended up in Dover where he worked sifting ashes in the Dockyards. At least he was fed and eventually given a chest in which to hold his books. He stayed for three years, and received instruction in Hebrew from a local Rabbi, which was probably more important to him than his pay of 2s 4d a day. His time in Chester, a few years later, was less distinguished. He was a complete nuisance and upset the residents by wandering through the streets, constantly blowing a ram's horn. Although his favourite author was Homer, he particularly enjoyed singing psalms in Hebrew, whilst accompanying himself on a Welsh harp which he had been given and repaired.

He spent a lot of time living on the streets of Liverpool, where he was a familiar figure, always with a book under his arm, not noticing or speaking to anyone. Dic was found on St. George's Pier Head by the radical poet and abolitionist, William Roscoe, who was fascinated by the books spilling out of his clothes and then shocked by his ability to hold an informed conversation about ancient linguistics. Roscoe wrote a biography of him and went on to give him a small allowance which brought him some stability for a while - and a room on Midghall Street. With his support, some of his writing was published, though it was all rather esoteric – including, for example, a Latin Treatise on the music and accents of the Hebrew language. But soon he was tramping around the countryside again.

He had little regard for his personal appearance which was described as *'disgusting and offensive.'* It was said that he was *'filthy in the extreme and his hands resemble in colour the back part of a sole,'* which has always been an image that has appealed to me. His clothes were threadbare and included *'a nasty rag, which may once have been white, and is probably still intended to represent a shirt.'* His clothes were stuffed with books,

'surrounding him in successive layers, so that he was literally a walking library. These books all occupied their proper stations, being placed higher or lower according as their size suited the conformation of his body, so that he was acquainted with each, and could bring it out when wanted, without difficulty.'

He turned up at the Beaumaris Eisteddfod in 1832 with an essay he had written in ancient Greek, on the three versions of the ancient harp. Since there was no competition requesting entries on this subject, he could not be awarded a prize. There was undoubtedly an obsessive element to his character. His magnum opus was his Welsh-Hebrew- Greek Dictionary, a book he worked on for two years and which had, by definition, a limited appeal. The only copy is now in the National Library in Aberystwyth where you can also find Dic Aberdaron's handwritten autobiography. Examples of his handwriting on their website bring you so much closer to this strange man.

There was, in some ways, a purity about his learning. It was pure in the sense that it was learning for its own sake because it benefited no one, least of all Dic. He learnt all those ancient languages which he was never able to use and acquired knowledge that he could never successfully share. Some regarded him as shiftless, with only a partial intellect *'displaying the most remarkable want of capacity on every other subject.'* He received much more generous understanding – and freedom - than perhaps he would have received today, when he would have been assessed, judged and treated. But in his own time his oddness brought with it a sense of mystery. Certainly the press were fascinated by what he represented. It was as if he had been touched by a divine influence which set him apart from others. They were wary of him as a consequence. There are elements that we can see in him that might today support a diagnosis of autism or Asperger's Syndrome. He was argumentative and difficult and not too keen on other people. And perhaps in a way, his talents were a curse – a barrier to proper engagement with the world and with other people.

The grave of Dic Aberdaron

In later life he returned frequently to St Asaph. Bishop Carey was very supportive and in fact was ready to do more for him, had not Dic been so independent. He used to lodge at the back of the George Inn in High Street, and it was there that he died in December, 1843 as penniless and alone as he had lived, and was buried in St Asaph Parish Churchyard.

He was an important and unusual figure in his own time but is generally forgotten today, unless you are studying the work of R.S. Thomas, who wrote a poem about him. He is, however, remembered on a gravestone provided by residents of St Asaph, which you can find quite easily, lying flat in the grass close by the railings, where there is a recently installed blue plaque, on the corner of Lower Street.

Swansea
Phoebe Phillips and her sisters 1870

The Bleeding Stone of Adulam

Adulam Baptist Chapel on Cefn Road is an uncompromising block of rendered grime, stranded on the east side of Swansea. It may squat on a bleak hillside forever blasted by cruel winds, but it does enjoy fine views down to Jersey Marine. Adulam is less important than it once was and the graves which remain belong to people who have long ago departed into a historical silence. But their stories will always have the power to touch us, once we know them. And none can reach us in the terrible way that the Phillips grave does. Look at the gravestone and you can see that it bleeds.

The Bleeding Stone of Adulam

168

No one can be indifferent in the face of what it represents. It tells a story from over 150 years ago, but even the inevitable passage of time cannot diminish that family tragedy. The gravestone was placed there by John and Eliza Phillips who lived at Halfway in Llansamlet, between Neath and Swansea, in 1870. The gravestone, inscribed in Welsh, remembers their three daughters, Phoebe fourteen, Emma twelve and Amelia seven, who drowned together in what was described at the time as a *'melancholy accident...a heart-rending scene, one of the most distressing incidents we have had to record.'* But then, how else could you describe it?

15 August 1870 seems to have been a pleasant day and offered the chance of some summer freedom for the girls, an adventure certainly, but with a purpose that would make Mam pleased – to collect some mussels for tea. They called to invite their cousin next door to come with them but their aunt, Tamar Davies, refused to let her accompany them.

Harvesting mussels wasn't really something they did. Phoebe had been twice before, but it was the first time for Emma and Amelia. They ran excitedly down to the shore between Port Tennant and Crymlin Burrows in the early evening and Phoebe took them out to an extensive sandbank called the Dulridge Bank, about half a mile off shore, which at low tide sat about 6 feet above the level of the beach. The locals knew that this substantial feature channelled the water as the tide came in and very quickly created a turbulent, racing current of terrible violence and power. But these were children and no one had told them.

There were other people down there too, that evening. A French seaman, Joseph Corin, had gone for a walk along the shore from his mooring in Swansea and in the peace of that late summer's afternoon had laid down in the grass on the dunes and fallen asleep.

He was awoken by screams, for whilst the girls collected the mussels and laughed and giggled, the water had risen around them.

When they looked up, they saw they were trapped on the wrong side of churning and dangerous currents. They ran up and down the rapidly diminishing sandbank, waving their cockle baskets and screaming as the water rose quickly around them.

Soon, there were over one hundred people there watching this terrible thing unfold, unable to do anything. They watched Corin throw off his clothes and dive into the cold water. They watched him swim through the current but saw that he couldn't climb up on to the sandbank. They heard Constable Flynn who, attracted by the noise, immediately called for a boat. They saw men running everywhere trying, and failing, to find one. They heard that William Thomas, landlord of *The Vale of Neath* public house in Port Tennant, had borrowed a horse from Mr Gould, the local farmer. They saw that it refused to enter the sea and that a second horse was brought, which was persuaded to ride off into the tide.

Of course, all this took a long time.

The horse was joined by a group of men from the Port Tennant Copper Works, who rushed into the water too. One of them, a moulder called Enright, grabbed hold of Phoebe and swam back with her, with every intention of going back for the others, but the current was too strong and the girl sank. When she surfaced she was caught by William Thomas, who then turned the horse towards the shore. The poor animal, however, was exhausted and reared up in the sea before it fell backwards on its two riders, and was dragged away by the tide.

This left William Thomas in a terrible situation, struggling for his own life in the water, whilst trying to save Phoebe. The description of what happened in the newspapers is heart breaking. *The child, naturally terrified, clung so tightly round his neck as to nearly choke him. He with difficulty unfastened her grasp, and held her at arm's length, himself growing rapidly exhausted.*

Phoebe, crying out for her sisters left behind, soon became convinced that that he was deliberately abandoning her.

She cried piteously not to leave her and made frantic clutches at him. After repeated struggles she again got hold of him round the neck, and again nearly choked him with the deadly tenacity of her hold. Again he thrust her from him, himself half-drowned and almost powerless, and again she closed upon him in an embrace of death.

But what was he to do? The sense of self-preservation is paramount within us all. Readers of the newspaper might have speculated upon their own bravery in such circumstances, but deep within themselves they might have understood how they would have reacted in such a situation.

With a last effort he tore her arms away from his neck, and pushed her off, swimming away from her for his life, feeling, as he left her, the clutch of her fingers at the sleeves of his shirt. On glancing back he saw her arms and hands just above the water, waving wildly about, and the tide carried her away, never to be seen any more alive.

Such powerful writing. It might be fanciful in places, but you can see how readers would have been so moved by both the description and the dilemma. William Thomas was picked up, *nearly insensible and quite exhausted,* by James Brown, who had come out on a horse borrowed from Mr. Roberts, formerly of *The Cuba Hotel* and was, with difficulty, brought ashore, hanging on to the animal's tail, *both horse and men having to do battle for their lives with the surging current.*

And all the time, Emma and Amelia were still running up and down what was left of the sandbank in frantic terror, screaming for their sister and watching her disappear forever beneath the grey water. Men tried desperately to reach them but to no avail and the spectators could only watch in horror as the inexorable tide submerged the sandbank. *Swimmer after swimmer was hurled back by the force of the waves.* Eventually, Joseph Corin reached the bank, but too late to save the children, *who had stood their ground bravely against the rising tide, till the water had reached their armpits, crying all the while piteously for help as they saw the unavailing efforts that were being made to bring them succour.*

They were washed away.

When Corin returned to shore he was in an exhausted condition, barely conscious. And he was alone.

The last that was seen of them was their little hands and arms waving wildly about, above the surface of the water, as they floated away in the distance, and were ultimately submerged and drowned.

On Tuesday morning the bodies were recovered. Phoebe and Emma had been deposited on the shore near Port Tennant by the receding tide. Amelia was found at Mumbles, on the opposite side of the bay. The inquest was held at the *Vale of Neath* where the bodies were brought. The parents were not at the inquest to listen to the details of their daughters' deaths. The bodies were identified by their aunt, Tamar Davies, who had not allowed her own daughter to go with them collecting mussels. The coroner Mr Strick was full of praise for the efforts made to rescue them by ordinary men putting themselves into life-threatening circumstances, whilst the police bemoaned the absence of a boat. Their efforts were described as being *above all praise.*

He reflected on the amount of time that had been lost. The girls had been fatally trapped very quickly indeed, but at least an hour had elapsed between the time the children were first seen and the moment when they were eventually submerged and swept away. If a boat had been available they would probably have been saved. Indeed, if the rescue had started sooner, before the water became too deep, they might have survived. Strick agreed that everyone did their best, but he did regret the loss of the horse, offered up so nobly. And they were expensive things, horses. This one was worth about £16. Mr Strick felt there should be a collection to reimburse Mr Gould for his loss and he was happy to offer the first contribution.

Very soon the necessary sum of £16 had been raised.

172

Trealaw, Rhondda
Daniel Thomas 1884

They come! They come! Their comrades true

Daniel Thomas in Trealaw

Daniel Thomas was a hero. He was born in January 1849; his father was a mine owner and he was educated by Mr Lloyd of Pontypridd, *'a gentleman who has trained for colliery management the majority of the Glamorgan colliery managers.'* Daniel was described as self-willed and decisive.

After serving as assistant to his father in the management of Brithwennydd Colliery, he succeeded him as manager in 1872. Daniel always knew the price of coal; Victorian industry and enterprise were paid for with the lives of miners. Theirs was a perilous occupation, followed by those with fragile lives.

On 11 April 1877 at the Tynewydd pit, a miner inadvertently hacked his way into the flooded workings of an abandoned colliery. There was a catastrophic inundation. Four miners were instantly drowned, others were trapped. Four were recovered on the first day of the rescue operation, although three rescuers died. But five others remained trapped underground. Their plight seized the popular imagination. There were daily reports of their plight in newspapers across the country. The Home Secretary gave daily progress reports to the House of Commons. The *Pontypool Free Press* reported that the Queen had '*constantly telegraphed for fresh information, in which anxiety she was joined by all classes throughout the country.*'

The five men had no food and only filthy water to drink. Initially they ate the wax dripping from their candles for a few days until the profound darkness of the flooded pit enveloped them. They could hear their colleagues digging but could not communicate with them and the water continued to rise around them as they waited. Soon it was up to their chins as they prayed and sang hymns, hammering on the coal face as much as they could with their picks. One of them was David Hughes, 14 years old; his father and brother had already drowned.

The rescue was led with considerable skill and expertise by Daniel Thomas and his brother Edmund. They went down the shaft and remained below throughout the operation, encouraging the diggers '*by their presence and example.*' Miners told reporters that '*it was the confidence that they felt in these two brothers which gave them courage to volunteer…and face the perils of water and fire and suffocation.*' They had huge problems to deal with – 113 feet of rock and coal had to be removed to reach the trapped men. Eventually a group of diggers led by Isaac Pride reached them and they were dragged out, weak and incoherent. They had been trapped for 10 days.

Queen Victoria subscribed £50 to the Tynewydd disaster fund and created a new order of merit. She declared that

'the Albert Medal, hitherto only bestowed for gallantry in saving life at sea, should be awarded for similar actions on land, and that the first medals awarded for this purpose should be conferred on the Tynewydd rescuer.'

It was, briefly, a national event. There was a song, *'The Gallant Men of Wales,'* sung at a Crystal Palace fete in aid of the Tynewydd Inundation Fund.

> *Dark, dark! No food! And higher still*
> *The hungry waters rose!*
> *But hark! A knocking at their tomb!*
> *A sound of mighty blows!*
> *The little lad wakes from his dreams,*
> *The bowed men hold their breath.*
> *They come! They come! Their comrades true-*
> *To rescue them from death.*

A reporter confirmed that some of the fund would be spent supporting the youngest survivor.

'I was much struck with the delicate and what I may truly call the refined look of the boy David Hughes who is only 14 years old and will be sent to school, as his education has hitherto been much neglected.'

Perhaps he was rescued from the pit for a second time.

Daniel Thomas and Isaac Pride received the Albert Medal First Class in a ceremony at the Mansion House in Pontypridd. Others received Second Class medals, including Edmund and other colliery owners and managers. Daniel also received the medal of the Knights Templars of Jerusalem and the medal of the Humane Society.

Daniel Thomas became a local hero. A mine owner perhaps - but one of their own. *The Western Mail* would later say that he *won the affection of a large section of the workmen by his considerate treatment of all in his employ. He differed from most colliery proprietors by taking a*

175

practical and leading part in the management of his collieries. Colliers in the remotest workings never knew what moment of the day Mr Thomas would visit them. He ever took the lead in his own collieries in the performance of hazardous undertakings.

His bravery, they said, '*bordered on recklessness.*'

There was a disastrous explosion in the Dinas Steam Coal Colliery on the 13th January, 1879, when many miners were entombed. The colliery was virtually destroyed and ready to be abandoned. Thomas, however, leased the colliery and made his first task the recovery of the bodies of the men. By the time of Thomas' death, 49 had been recovered, leaving only six still to be found. He was also able to restore production at the colliery, thus boosting employment. He paid out over £5,000 a month in wages.

But in the Naval Steam Coal Colliery in Penygraig, his luck ran out. There had already been a huge explosion there in December 1880, when over a hundred miners were killed. Reports described the discovery of 16 dead miners in a kneeling position, '*death having come to them while they were engaged in prayer.*' The pit's reputation as '*a fiery one*' was seen again in January 1884. There was another tremendous explosion, so fierce that a child was thrown out of bed over half a mile away. The manager had ordered a controlled explosion on a Sunday morning to shatter rocks, but it all went horribly wrong. '*A straight white column shot up from the pit's mouth as from a canon, its centre full of fire.*'

Men rushed to the pit to see what could be done. Daniel Thomas arrived and took a party down to look for survivors. Thankfully there had not been many in the pit at the time of the explosion, but eleven men were unaccounted for.

Thomas led the way carefully through the workings. They found the bodies of men and horses but the air was thick and deadly. Thomas gave the instruction to turn back. But it was too late. He and two colleagues, Edward Watkins and Thomas 'Double Strength' Davies, were overcome by the afterdamp – a deadly mixture of carbon monoxide, carbon dioxide and nitrogen.

When his death was announced, there was an out-pouring of grief. *'Men, whose blue-scarred faces told of a lifetime spent in the Rhondda mines, wept like children.'* His remains *'were placed in the dining -room and the canvas was then opened. The features bore the expression of calm repose. Thick dust was in his beard, and his face was begrimed.'*

Leave Porth and drive further into the Rhondda along the A4058, to the large cemetery at Trealaw. It is easy to find the impressive memorial to the bravery of Daniel Thomas, situated along the road on the right hand side as you enter.

The short white marble cenotaph has three engraved panels with a black-painted bronze bust of Thomas by W Davies of Caerphilly. It is a profile which suggests nobility and compassion and displays proudly his medals for bravery. The monument was designed with the front facing the valley where the mines used to be and which is now green and peaceful. Such memories are disappearing as we bury the past beneath the tarmac but we must forget neither the heroism nor the sense of duty that led all those years ago to this shortened cenotaph in the cemetery at Trealaw.

Wrexham
Elihu Yale
1721

Much good, some ill, he did; so hope all's even

In the graveyard of the fine parish church of St Giles in Wrexham you will find the substantial tomb of Elihu Yale, who was buried here in 1721 and has a world-famous American university named after him. It is large and unmistakeable, sitting close to the porch on the right hand side. It has on it an interesting biographical epitaph, allegedly written by Yale himself.

Born in America, in Europe bred
In Africa travell'd and in Asia wed
Where long he liv'd and thriv'd; In London dead.
Much good, some ill, he did; so hope all's even
And that his soul thro' mercy's gone to Heaven.
You that survive and read this tale, take care
For this most certain exit to prepare
Where, blest in peace, the actions of the just
Smell sweet and blossom in the silent dust.

His is a strange and unexpected story, one that challenges our modern sensibilities and still causes real discomfort. Elihu Yale was certainly a man of his times, but as a sometimes brutal slave trader, his legacy is unsettling.

His family had been part of the Puritan migration to Massachusetts and had settled in Boston. Elihu Yale was born there in 1649 but, even though his grandmother was married to the governor of Newhaven, the family returned to London in 1672, finding the regime of the colony rather grim.

Yale never returned to America and spent much of his adult life working in India for the British East India Company, rising steadily to a senior position, which enabled him to amass a considerable personal fortune through a range of corrupt practices. He became the governor of St George Fort in Madras (now Chennai) marrying his predecessor's widow, Catherine. He also kept two mistresses, one of whom, Catherine Nicks, was a notorious diamond smuggler.

St Giles' Church, Wrexham

It is impossible to establish just how much money he accumulated in India, through numerous illicit activities including diamond smuggling. Yale also earned a great deal from his involvement in the slave trade.

He sold a large number of slaves to the settlement of St Helena and introduced a regulation that every European ship leaving Madras must carry with it a minimum of ten slaves to be sold,

179

which he provided. In 1687, in just one month, 665 people were trafficked out of India. When demand for slaves increased, the traders began kidnapping young children. Yale himself was notoriously brutal. Slaves were whipped and branded. He '*hanged his groom for riding out with his horse for two or three days to take the air without his leave.*'

His lasting legacy in Madras was the building of a hospital in 1664 to care for the health of English families, soldiers and merchants, but his greatest motivation was always profit.

Yale was eventually removed from office in 1692, his habit of buying land for his own purposes using East India Company money proving to be a step too far. Catherine had left him earlier, in 1688, and Yale removed her name from his will, substituting the words, 'my wicked wife.'

He was detained in India until he was eventually allowed to leave in 1699. Back in England he lived quietly, dividing his time between London and the family property in Plas Grono near Wrexham, which had been acquired by his great grandfather David Yale, and is now part of the Erddig estate, a National Trust property. Plas Grono was demolished in 1876.

Despite his fall from grace in Madras, he was still ridiculously wealthy. It is believed that he acted as the first auctioneer in England when he sold off some of his property; he had brought home so many possessions, he did not enough room for them in his house. After his death, seven separate auctions were required to dispose of his property. It included several hundred snuff boxes, 500 rings, 100 canes, 7,000 paintings and 116 pairs of cufflinks.

As he grew older, Yale devoted his time to the church and served as the high sheriff of Denbigh. Perhaps his Christian beliefs encouraged a time of reflection and regret, who can say? He was certainly a benefactor of St Giles' Church, donating devotional paintings. He paid for a new gallery across the east end of the nave which '*contained several pews, of which the six front ones were to be at the disposal of Mr Yale, and the remainder at the disposal of the Churchwardens.*' In 1718, he became dissatisfied with the position of this gallery and so removed it and reinstalled it at the west end of the nave. It is on occasions like this that you may be reminded of the old Welsh proverb – '*The closer to the church, the further from God.*'

It was in that same year that Yale created his place in history. He had previously presented a set of thirty-two valuable books to the Collegiate College at Saybrook in Connecticut, but when it relocated to Newhaven, he received a letter from Cotton Mather, the religious writer, in Connecticut.

Mather had written *Magnalia Christi Americana* about God's chosen people – the puritans – and their heroic story, '*fleeing from the deprivations of Europe to the American strands*' where they '*irradiated an Indian wilderness.*' He was not too proud however, to accept European money and asked Yale to help the school, now that it had moved. Yale responded by sending a gift of nine bales of goods, together with 417 books and a portrait of King George I. The sale of the goods raised money for a new building, creating the basis on which the university was founded, the third oldest institute of higher education in America. It later changed its name in recognition of this gift in 1745 to Yale University. It may be interesting to note that, just before his death, Yale sent out a further miscellany of goods for them, though they were, allegedly, lost in transit.

Yale was 73 when he died in London in July 1721 and was buried in St Giles' in Wrexham, where that solid tomb still squats.

For a while there was a desire to promote the links between the University and Wrexham. It was certainly something about which the town was proud and the university liked the idea of its Old World origins. There were frequent exchanges and visits, enthusiastically reported in the press.

On a visit in 1874, members of the university found that those words of the epitaph had eroded so badly that they arranged for the letters to be recut. In 1900 American visitors expressed some dissatisfaction with the tomb and decided to send over a new memorial *"of elaborate design showing Yale lying at rest under an open canopy worked in stone and marble.'* The plan, perhaps thankfully, came to nothing, as did the scheme to take the tomb and his remains back to America. In 1902, on the bicentenary of the founding of the college in Saybrook, Yale University raised £400 to restore the north porch of the church and representatives laid wreaths on his tomb. In 1918 a stone from the west tower was taken to America and inserted in the walls of a new university building as a physical representation of the links between them.

But the interest faded as times changed. His legacy began to conflict with the modern world and eventually those links proved to be an embarrassment. As an enthusiastic slave trader and fraudster, Elihu Yale was no longer the sort of person with whom a university might like to celebrate a relationship, since he hardly complies with Yale's values. After all, he is regarded in India as a *'arrogant ruthless braggart…who cheated both his employers and the people of India.'* After complaints from students in 2007, a portrait of Yale with a dark-skinned servant wearing a metal collar was removed from a wall in the university.

Yale University has already changed the name of one of its constituent colleges that had been named after an advocate of slavery. They might well move on to the renaming of the university as a whole.

And that epitaph on his tomb he allegedly wrote himself? Well, the last two lines are, perhaps typically, lifted from a seventeenth century poem by James Shirley, *Death, the Leveller.*

If you examine the epitaph closely, you will notice the regret and anxiety of lines 4 and 5. *'Much good, some ill, he did; so hope all's even / And that his soul thro mercy's gone to Heaven.'* Those words are, I think, particularly revealing.

Finally

People who are interested in cemeteries have a name; they are called Taphophiles. Please understand though, their compulsion might have a clever name, but it isn't dry and dusty and neither is it about death. Far from it. Their compulsion is simply for life, and a need to understand how our ancestors, who weren't really a great deal different to ourselves, lived theirs, They felt the same emotions, they had the same hopes and dreams. They were just like us, in fact, except they wore different clothes and had technology that was far less complicated than ours.

This is the most important thing a taphophile can teach you about gravestones; that they embody people just like ourselves, who might have experienced joy and unhappiness, in a life that may have been well lived, or may have been defined by sadness and disappointment. And perhaps now, that life is represented by nothing at all, other than by a fading piece of chiselled stone.

The stone pictured here, close to where I live, carries a horrific story, about real people and real history and yet it is a story that is barely known.

It maps out in awful detail the unthinkable tragedy of the family of Richard and Hannah Rees. Imagine their sorrow, if any of us are capable of such a thing. In a period of 20 years, between 1865 and 1885, they had eleven children, all of whom died in childhood and are remembered on this single stone. It is a horrible register of anguish.

Richard two years old, Mary Anne two years old, Maria Jane fifteen years old, David two years old, Richard six years old, David one year old, Elizabeth ten years old, William and Thomas (twins) one year old, Elizabeth Ann and Maria Jane (twins) three months old.

Don't dare tell me this was normal; don't dare tell me that they got used to it or that in those days life was cheap; don't dare tell me that they were unlucky. This was Richard and Hannah's life, the only life they had, and the emotions this ageing memorial represents are unimaginable.

Is it really possible for any of us to pass this gravestone by on the other side, once we realise that this is, now, the only way those little lives will ever be remembered? Lives that had such potential, but were never fulfilled, and the deaths that must have shaped Richard and Hannah's world.

That is why graves and cemeteries are important. They bring us history that is unfiltered but too-frequently overlooked. And they have an inherent contradiction too, for these representations of death bring history to life. The stones of Wales remind us of lives that we can never live, but they are lives that can teach us so much, once we are prepared to listen.

Geoff Brookes

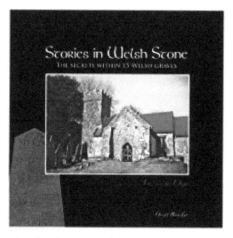

You might also be interested in my first book on this subject titled *Stories in Welsh Stone* ISBN 978 0 95587350 8. To obtain this, please visit Amazon.

Lightning Source UK Ltd.
Milton Keynes UK
UKHW050300150722
405862UK00006B/237